Table of content

Foreword

A family dog as a future life com ⌐⌐⌐⌐⌐⌐⌐⌐⌐ ⌐ght. However, despite all the euphoria mily, several important aspects should not be overlooked. ... , you might not consider all of them. Nevertheless, one should think about it seriously before the wish for one's own dog is turned into reality. I am aware that there are already innumerable books which are dedicated to many different topics around dogs. However, I have not found one that summarizes all the questions that arise, especially for newcomers to dogs. And there are many questions concerning the decision to get a dog for the very first time. So I decided to create a guidebook that deals with the topic "My first dog" as a whole.

My guide is aimed primarily at all those dog lovers who for the first time in their lives are planning to take in a dog as a family member. The diverse thought-provoking suggestions and hints deal precisely with this plan and are intended to be a decision-making aid. If the decision has been made to take in a dog, this book provides numerous tips for getting off to the best possible start and for living together in the future. As we took in our first dog as a puppy, this book focuses on that situation, but the guide is just as useful for taking in an older dog. In addition, there are also many interesting topics for those who already live with a dog of their own and want to expand their knowledge.

Note for international readers: As I live in Germany, some of the contents of my guide refer specifically to my place of residence. This applies, for example, to the chapter "Costs," in which the expenditure of the EU currency the Euro is indicated, or the chapter "Obligations and Recommendations," in which I deal with the topics of the obligation to register, regulations about dogs being on a leash, insurance and legal consequences in Germany. However, it should be easy to find out the information for different parts of the world by an internet research on the respective countries or by asking experts from your home country.

Introduction

Just like many other dog lovers, I once arrived at a point in life where I would like to have a dog of my own. Apart from this thought, however, I had little plan at that time on how to deal with this wish and what I had to consider, take into account and prepare for. After all, there are quite a lot of questions around life with a dog and I got the answers from just as many sources. These included, for example, personal conversations with dog-experienced people and dog trainers, reading various literature and an extensive search on the internet.

My guidebook is intended to reduce this large number of research sources to a minimum and to cover all the basic and some detailed questions in a single book. As mentioned in the preface, my focus is on the "family dog" that is considered a companion. By "companion," I mean the dog as a living being to whom one likes to dedicate one's time, to whom one gives one's love and attention, who one cares for and looks after - in good times and in bad!

In chapters 1 to 7, I mainly give general information based on internet research, books, and conversations with longtime dog owners. I have researched various special topics on expert pages on the internet. The corresponding sources can be found under "Research Sources" at the end of the book. In chapters 1 to 7, I also write about my personal experiences, which are inserted alongside relevant passages. In the 8th and last chapter, everything revolves around my individual insights and experiences with our Bernese Mountain Dog Merlin.

But I think that in the individual chapters all those aspects are addressed which are helpful for planning to adopt a family dog and for the future living together with it. On the broad topic of "training", I recommend purchasing additional literature that deals exclusively with dog training. By contacting a dog trainer, one can get valuable tips if the dog has a difficult character and needs individual training.

When I give recommendations, nobody should feel obliged to follow them. Just like every human being, every dog is fundamentally different. And so living together with a dog is always very individual - but you will experience this yourself with your first own dog!

CHAPTER 1: The first thing you should think about

One rarely comes "all of a sudden" to want to own a dog, and that is a good thing. The decision for a dog as a new member of the family should be very well thought out and planned. Positive motives for the desire for a dog can range from a general love of animals to the joy of living together with a dog to the decision to offer a poor dog - whether young or old - a good home. Whatever your personal reason, you can be sure that there is no more loyal friend than a dog!

For a dog owner, there are some more positive aspects, for example, you spend more time in the fresh air by walking your dog. This not only keeps the dog fit, but also you. At the same time, you can - if you want to - easily get in contact with other people who are dog owners and dog friends. In the following, I will also mention a few negative motives, even if they may sound a bit harsh. However, I think that they should be addressed. I am convinced anyway that your desire for a dog should not be influenced by how the outside world perceives or should perceive you and your dog. A negative motive would be, for example, that you consider a dog as a fashion accessory or as a status symbol. Smaller breeds in particular - for example, those that fit into a handbag - are often taken in because they have been seen on TV with some celebrity or on the internet by an "influencer."

Also, you should not bring a Husky into your home if you hardly do any sports, have little time for sports or prefer to do the sport alone. Just because a husky is known to be very active and sporty, nobody will think you are a sportsman because of your dog. Furthermore, a dog should not be used to supposedly boost self-confidence or self-esteem. Often enough, powerful Rottweilers or Pitbulls and their masters and mistresses give exactly this impression.

You should also be willing to organize your leisure activities around your dog. If your friends are having a party on New Year's Eve, then you should either stay at home or only join it if you looked for a dog sitter. Because New Year's Eve is the most terrible night of the year for your dog and therefore he should not be alone. Some hobbies, such as playing drums or a loud instrument, are definitely not dog-friendly either. Dogs hear many times more intensively than we humans, they even hear frequencies that are no longer perceptible to the human ear. Noise or loud music is therefore quite the worst thing in the world for him - right after being alone!

In general, you should arrange your leisure activities so that they are dog-friendly. This includes, for example, avoiding going out for a beer or two immediately after work or spending several hours in a gym. After all, your dog is waiting at home eagerly for you and for you to feed and walk him. If you have children, you should never give them a dog just because they are constantly begging for one. Smaller children in particular can never take care of the new pet, and therefore the whole  care, as well as the education, will be exclusively with the parents, older siblings or other adult family members. The worst thing would be if then no one has time to take care of the dog, except to provide him with food and let him outside from time to time to do his business. However, your dog will not only suffer if you lock him up alone for hours every day for lack of time or to protect the children (or rarely, to protect the dog from the children). Your dog suffers in the same way if he is constantly bossed around by different people while the children are at home.

General requirements

In addition to your personal reasons for the planned addition of a dog, you should consider the following criteria in your decision.

Family status

If you live alone, you can make the decision for a dog yourself. However, if you live with a partner or have a family of your own, it is important to clarify whether everyone can imagine a dog as a new family member and whether they agree with the addition of one. If your partner or someone else in the family is afraid of dogs, this must be discussed. And it has to be clarified whether this fear can be overcome and the person involved can imagine building a trusting relationship with a dog. In addition, it should be checked out whether an allergy to animal hair, in particular, a dog hair allergy, is present. If this is the case, one must decide for better or worse and consider an alternative pet.

Housing conditions

Housing conditions are another important aspect when planning to purchase a dog. If you own a condominium or even your own house, you don't have to ask anyone whether it is permitted to keep a dog there. However, if you live in a rented apartment or house, it is essential to clarify in advance whether you can keep a dog in your home. If this is not the case, but the wish for a dog is nevertheless present, then a change of apartment (as we have done) will probably not be rejected. It is important that dog keeping is explicitly allowed in the new rental contract and that this is recorded in writing.

If your apartment is in a multi-party house and you want to have a bigger dog, a lift would be good. A puppy/young dog should not climb too many stairs because of the not yet finished bone growth. An older dog, on the other hand, will find it difficult to climb stairs sooner or later. Carrying a large (and heavy) dog up and down stairs several times a day is a rather bad solution, because it is either not feasible at all or can only be done with great physical effort. The living conditions also have an effect on the size of the dog in question. Temperamental breeds like the German Shepherd, Border Collie, Australian Shepherd, Husky and so on will not feel comfortable in a small apartment. However, this does not mean that a large dog such as a St. Bernard, Newfoundland, Great Dane or Wolfhound cannot be kept in an apartment. What is important in this case is that you regularly take your dog out into the fresh air so that he can get enough exercise outside and explore or sniff the area. We always call walking "reading the newspaper".

If you are not very active yourself, then you should not include particularly active and intelligent breeds on the shortlist. This includes all breeds known as hunting, herding, driving and working dogs.

Living conditions

If you want to have a dog, you should be prepared to put aside your own needs for the dog. This means, for example, that you cannot just spend the evening or weekend comfortably on the couch, but you must also walk the dog in between - no matter if it rains or snows. In the same way, holidays have to be planned differently if you do not want to give your dog up during this time but take him with you. A holiday with a dog promotes your bond with him and his with you. Speaking of bonding: are you prepared to commit yourself to a dog for several years? Because if you take a puppy, you will share your life with this dog - depending on the breed - for the next 10 to 15 years. You should generally think about whether you have the necessary time for a dog.

Dogs are pack animals and have difficulty coping with being completely alone. Working people should therefore clarify in advance whether it is possible to take your dog to work. If it is not possible to take the dog to work, you should know someone who can either look after the dog and walk him during your absence or maybe even take him to your home during the day.

On average, an adult dog sleeps 12 to 14 hours a day. But even if he sleeps most of the day, he should not be left alone for a whole working day. It would be good to check on him during this period and perhaps give him the opportunity to do his business outside. It can also happen that the dog breaks something in your (long) absence from home out of boredom or annoys the neighbors by constant barking or howling.

A further question to be clarified is how or with whom you can accommodate your dog, if you become ill and cannot take care of him for a certain period of time. A solution should also be found in the case that you plan a holiday without a dog. Either someone from your circle of friends or acquaintances can then take over the dog or you can ask for a good dog person in your area. Another solution would be to place the dog temporarily in an animal shelter - some shelters offer their own boarding places for this purpose. If the dog is given into the hands of a stranger, he should definitely be chipped and the chip number should be recorded online - just in case he runs away while walking. A dog that is chipped is NOT automatically registered in an animal identification database or in a pet register! You will find the details of the procedure for registration in chapter 2 under "Chip". You should also not only look at your current living conditions, but think about whether your personal circumstances could possibly change in the future due to a new job, a change of residence or a new family situation.

Attitude to cleanliness

One thing must be clear to you: a dog causes more or less dirt depending on breed, size and coat condition. After a walk in the rain or sleet, the paws are definitely dirty, and after a walk in the snow, at least wet. In this case, your car and/or your floor at home may become covered with corresponding traces of dirt or small puddles of water. This should be as unproblematic for you as various hair accumulations in the home.

A dog, like any pet with fur, loses more or less hair (whether it has long or short) and these will regularly "decorate" your apartment or house. With our Bernese mountain dog, the hair loss is not only very large in the spring, but also partly during the year and especially when the outside temperatures rise. He then "airs out" his thick winter coat, so to speak, and leaves behind a more extensive amount of hair in the house than is normally the case due to the change of coat.

Speaking of hairs, these are often mistakenly described as the cause of allergies. However, a dog allergy is a hypersensitivity of the immune system to certain substances released by dogs in saliva, urine and glandular secretions. Contrary to popular belief, long-haired dogs actually cause fewer allergies than their short-haired counterparts. The reason: short-haired dogs are more affected by shedding than their long-haired counterparts.

Fortunately, there are several breeds that are suitable for dog lovers with allergies. Namely, unlike other dog breeds, these have hair - not fur. The significant difference: in the fur-bearer there is a change of coat from summer to winter and vice versa. Thus, he continuously loses his coat (with "contaminated" dandruff or saliva). The breeds with hair include, for example, the poodle and all variants of the so-called "water dogs" and also Havanese, Maltese, Bichon Frisé, Yorkshire Terrier as well as the Labradoodle and the Goldendoodle.

Regardless of the breed, having a dog means that you will have to spend several times a week cleaning your apartment/house. What you as a dog owner should not put a big priority on (anymore) as well: 100 percent clean clothes! I always say, you can recognize a dog owner by the fact that he never is absolutely spotless - especially when it comes to trousers and shoes.

CHAPTER 2: Other important issues

Dog experience

Please always remember that you have to get along with the dog of your choice. If you are an indulgent, inconsistent or insecure person, you should not get a dog of a breed known as temperamental or dominant. I would like to point out that no dog is born dominant or even aggressive. Some dog breeds such as Rottweilers, Shepherds, Dobermans or Pitbulls simply have a higher protective instinct and a lower threshold than, for example, a Golden Retriever or Labrador. Regardless of their nature, you should also ask yourself the question of whether you are able to cope with your dog's strength. This applies not only to yourself, but also to every member of your family and to every person who cares for your dog and takes him for walks. Especially when walking your dog, you or the respective dog handler must be able to control the situation at any time.

After all, the dog should not be able to drag you out into the street, if, for example, he sees a cat or another dog on the opposite side of the road. With a well-behaved dog, however, this situation should not occur anyway. (See chapter 6, "Education and behavior.") You should also consider whether your own temperament and that of your dog are compatible. If you prefer to live your life in a quiet and contemplative manner, a young, hectic, active dog will not suit you.

Costs

A dog as a companion gives a lot of pleasure, but his maintenance can also cause some costs during the course of his life. For this reason, you should ask yourself whether your financial position allows you to offer your four-legged friend everything he needs. In addition to the ongoing supply of food, you must also plan for the costs of the veterinarian, dog tax and dog insurance. If you assume that your dog will be with you for 10 to 15 years, the estimated expenses during this time can add up to 10,000 Euros.

These are the costs in the event that:
- your dog does not get complicated diseases,
- you do not give him exclusive collars, toys or dog beds,

- he is not placed in a good kennel for weeks every year, and
- he does not regularly receive private lessons in a professional dog school.

The (estimated) expenditure mentioned above is made up of:

- Aquisition: A dog from the shelter costs on average about 200 Euros, but for a pedigree dog from a recognized breeder, sometimes far more than 1,000 Euros have to be spent.
- Veterinarian: For a "healthy" dog, about 100 Euros per year are estimated (for example, for vaccinations to be updated and for deworming).
- Taxes: These depend on your place of residence and the breed, and cost between 20 and 100 Euros per year.
- Third-party insurance: This is highly recommended and costs about 100 Euros per year.
- Food: Depending on the size of your dog and the type of food, you should allow between 25 and 80 Euros per month.
- Accessories: If you provide your dog with only the most essential items (collar, leash, blanket), you should plan on about 100 Euros.

The above costs may be higher with the following factors:

- Attending a dog school or a dog psychologist: for this, the costs per hour can amount to 20 to 100 Euros.
- Use of a kennel: in case of holiday or illness, you should calculate daily costs of 15 to 50 Euros.
- Veterinarian: The costs for castration start at 250 Euros for a male and 650 Euros for a female. For larger operations, such as hip surgery, they are about 2,000 Euros, and for eye surgery, about 1,000 Euros.
- Accessories: For toys and special accessories, there are no upper limits to the prices. For example, a designer coat can cost as much as 500 Euros.

Obligations and recommendations

Besides good manners towards fellow humans, as a dog owner, nowadays one has to fulfill some (legal) obligations, which are described in more detail below. Please note that the statements refer to the situation in Germany, they are of course different in each country.

Import prohibition: In Germany, each state government must determine the respective rights and duties of dog owners. So the duties differ depending on the region. However, there are a few basic rules which every (future) dog owner should observe. According to the German Civil Code (BGB), the purchase of a dog is equated with the purchase of an object. Puppies are subject to a special protection here: only after eight weeks may they be separated from their mothers. You should also note that certain breeds may not be imported into Germany. Among others, this import prohibition includes the Pitbull Terrier, American Staffordshire Terrier, Staffordshire Bull Terrier, and Bull Terrier.

Obligation to register: You must register your dog in your town or municipality and pay the dog tax. Depending on the region and the number of dogs, the range is between 20 and 100 Euros per year, as mentioned above. Dogs with a specific purpose are exempt from the tax. These include guide and assistance dogs for the disabled, avalanche search dogs and guard dogs. The registration should take place between the day your four-legged friend moves in, and, at the latest, 3 months later. For large dogs and/or dogs of certain breeds (list dogs) there is a legal obligation to register (and to obtain permission) at the public order office. Please inquire at your local public order office whether your dog is affected by this and which requirements must be met.

Mandatory dog leashing: Depending on the place of residence, such a regulation is usually valid within the entire town/city area. In general, one should always pay attention to signs that say whether dogs are allowed there or not. In public places with many people, you should always take precautions to protect other passers-by such as pedestrians, cyclists, joggers, inline skaters, and horsemen. This includes leashing and possibly putting on a muzzle. However, the exact duties and rules always depend on the city in question.

Walking the dog / Duty to remove dog excrement: In some green areas, dogs are forbidden, so you should always pay attention to any signs. In Germany and Austria, the so-called dog excrement law applies. According to this law, excrement is regarded as contamination under the waste disposal law and must be removed. No matter if it's in green areas or on sidewalks, if you don't remove the excrement, you are breaking the law and are liable to prosecution.

Securing the dog in the car: In Germany, dogs are considered to be transported goods and should be transported in a car and secured accordingly. In the event of a sudden braking maneuver, an unsecured dog can become a life-threatening projectile that endangers the people in the car and himself. By the way, unlike when riding a bicycle, it is absolutely forbidden to let dogs run alongside the car.

Dog handling license/certificate of competence: In some countries and cities in Germany, you have to present a certificate of competence or a dog handler's license when an inspection is carried out by a police officer - especially if the dog is a listed breed. The certificate of competence is obtained through a one-off course that can be completed at a veterinarian's or veterinary office. The examination for the dog handler license is very extensive. In the practical part, the examiners observe dog and owner in typical everyday situations - in a café, when the dog is under the table and the waiter comes, when strolling in the pedestrian zone and when walking in the park without a leash. The dog must neither endanger people nor disturb the environment. In the theoretical part, the dog owner has to answer questions about dog behavior and dog education. The dog handler license is recognized in some German states as a proof of competence.

Chip: Your dog should or has to (depending on the place of residence) be chipped (electronically marked). Mostly it is a microchip which is injected under the skin on the left side of the neck. The chip enables the clear identification of your dog and is helpful in returning a lost dog to his owner. When travelling in other EU countries, a dog must be chipped. Please note that the chip is inserted by a veterinarian, but registration is not automatic afterwards. As already mentioned, the chip number (it is usually in the vaccination certificate of the dog) must always be registered by you!

In Germany, you can do this online and free of charge on the platforms www.tasso.net (International), www.findefix.com (Focus on Germany) or www.animaldata.com (Focus on Austria).

If you move or get a new phone number, you should also notify this change on the platform chosen for chip registration. An international but chargeable platform would be, for example, www.safepet.eu. If you are offered an animal with a vaccination certificate, and a chip number is entered into it, you can also search and check the microchip number on www.petmaxx.com.

Insurance: Depending on your place of residence, and generally highly recommended, is a liability insurance for your dog. You can either link this to your private liability or take out a separate policy. After all, it can always happen that your dog causes damage that in some cases cannot be paid for without insurance (for example, if your dog runs in front of a car and this results in an accident with personal injury or major property damage). To choose an insurance company, it is recommended that you either contact a trusted insurance broker or do your own research on the internet. There are many different types of insurance, which sometimes also include the dog breed. Further differences exist in the respective amount of cover, the deductible amount and how much rental property damage is insured. Some dog owners take out additional dog health insurance. There are variants with full coverage, with surgery coverage only or with accident coverage only. With this type of insurance, the insurance companies often include the respective dog breeds. We had already included dog health insurance for our dog Merlin at the puppy stage. But since we had to visit the vet with him during the first years of his life, and of course we submitted the bills to the insurance company, the insurance was cancelled after a few years. After that, we did not take out a new insurance. The decision for or against your own dog's health insurance has to be made by you.

Legal consequences: If you, as a dog owner, violate the aforementioned laws, you must expect a fine, and, in the worst case, even the removal of your dog. It's just as well to know: if your dog injures another dog because you have not fulfilled your duty of supervision, it can happen that you have to pay compensation for damages if you file a complaint.

CHAPTER 3: Thoughts for selection

Before you get into the question of which dog is best suited to you, you should know the following: don't just be influenced by the cute look, but also consider the typical requirements of a certain breed. These include, for example,

- a great eagerness to run (as in the Border Collie, Husky, Australian Shepherd, Golden Retriever, Dalmatian, German Shepherd and Doberman),
- a pronounced hunting instinct (as in the Beagle, Dachshund, German Wirehaired, Weimaraner, Setter and Terriers) or
- a high effort for grooming (as in the Afghan Hound, Bernese Mountain Dog, Saint Bernard, Newfoundland, Havanese, Spaniel).

If you are looking for a dog that is considered particularly suitable for families, these breeds come into consideration, for example: Beagle, Boxer, Bernese Mountain Dog, Collie, Dalmatian, French Bulldog, Golden Retriever, Irish Setter, Labrador, Magyar Vizsla, Newfoundland or Poodle. The mentioned breeds are also generally known to be very child-friendly and on top of that they are well suited for beginners. The same applies to the breeds Bichon Frisé, Bolognese, Chihuahua, English Bulldog, Maltese, Maltipoo, Pug dog, Shih Tzu, all Spaniel species, Spitz, West Highland Terrier and Yorkshire Terrier.

Please note: There is no ONE dog breed that can be defined as the perfect family dog for every family. To find the best, most family-friendly or child-friendly dog for you, you should always consider your individual needs and your current and future life situation. For living with a dog you have to define who is the main person responsible for the four-legged friend in the long run. Especially in a family, the person who actually wanted to take over the responsibility is not always the one who then mainly deals with the dog in the end. It is not in the nature of dogs to have several reference persons. One person in the household will eventually have a closer connection to the dog than all the others. With this in mind, the breed of dog should be chosen with the future caregiver in mind. There are many other criteria that influence the final decision. I would like to give you some food for thought on the ones listed below.

Age

Most people who want to take in a dog think of a puppy first. But does it necessarily have to be a puppy with whom you gain your first experience as a dog owner? There are older dogs, who, through no fault of their own, have lost their previous home, for example, because the owner has died or a life event has occurred that caused the dog to be abandoned. Some older dogs eke out an existence as strays and are caught without anyone ever asking about them. In some foreign shelters, stray dogs are very often given a certain period of time and the dog is put down when this period is over.

Thoughts about taking in a puppy

With puppies and young dogs, you should be aware that they require a lot of patience, time, energy, education, and, above all, good nerves. If you take in a puppy, you can assume that he is not house-trained and prefers to leave his puddles and feces on the carpet instead of leaving them in a place where you could simply wipe them away. You should therefore take a puppy out immediately after eating or drinking, and generally once every 2 hours or so, so that he can relieve himself. This way he should also be housebroken quickly.

You should be prepared for the fact that a puppy, like a toddler, might clear out the shelves, for example, or use shoes as chew bones, tear up cushions or bite off carpet fringes. And you should expect that every time a puppy is left alone in the house, it will be seen as a disaster - followed by other disasters, small or large. These include leaving feces around, and emptying trash cans and distributing the contents around the home. In addition, being alone at home could be commented on with persistent howling.

A puppy has no idea about education and about what his humans understand by living together harmoniously. He does not know what he is allowed to do and what he is not. Neither does he know which of his games are no longer fun for his owner.

If you want to get a puppy because you have small children and an adult dog seems too dangerous for you, then you should know the following: the milk teeth of puppies are extremely sharp, and dogs naturally use their teeth when playing! So it's not surprising that these milk teeth can often leave deep scratches and even bleeding marks on you or your children. In this case, however, you should not  become hysterical and immediately label the dog as "biting." When a large puppy is playing with a small child, it can happen that a not yet stable child is pushed in the hustle and bustle and falls over. However, this should not immediately cause horror with parents and one should therefore not immediately accuse the dog of malice.

If you decide on a mixed-breed puppy, you should always be flexible regarding his final size and appearance. It often happens that a mixed-breed dog then becomes larger (or remains smaller) than you originally expected. If the new family member is a purebred dog like a St. Bernard puppy, it is clear from the beginning that this initially small woolly guy will one day become a giant. Not only the appearance of the adult dog, but also the later characteristics, sometimes cause unexpected or unpleasant surprises. In purebred dogs, the characteristics can be predicted approximately, although they are not set in stone.

With a mixed-breed puppy, the estimation of the characteristics becomes more difficult. If you acquire such a puppy yourself, you will not know how he will develop. As an adult dog, he may have a strong hunting, protection or herding instinct, and you may not want to have a dog with such characteristics. No matter which puppy it will be, whether purebred or mixed breed, it is undoubtedly a great pleasure to accompany him on his way to becoming a real dog, to play with him and to discover the world together with him. But you should not forget that, especially in the first months, it will be a lot of work and an immense effort for you, for the puppy to grow up to be a safe, well educated, unproblematic, and, finally, wonderful family member.

Thoughts about taking in an old dog

If you prefer to take in an older/old dog, then take your time when choosing. The best thing is to visit an animal shelter, an animal welfare association or an emergency center for dogs and get detailed information, because there you will also get honest and competent advice. When choosing an older/old dog, you have a definite advantage: you know who you are getting, especially with regard to size and character, and can better decide whether this dog with his individual character, temperament and characteristics exactly fits you and your current and future life situation.

An old dog is also usually already house-trained and doesn't get any stupid ideas. He knows his environment (for example, the noises at home and outside), is more or less educated and - depending on the breed - does not need as much exercise as a young one. Unfortunately, the fairy tale is often told that an old dog does not adapt to a new environment and cannot adapt to a new family. But that is absolute nonsense!

If you decide to get an old dog, you will be surprised how quickly he will settle into your home! It can happen so quickly that you and your dog will feel like you've spent your whole life together. Old dogs have a very special charisma. An additional argument for choosing an old dog is that you can spare him from growing old in the shelter and give him a new home. Unfortunately, it is often the case that the most wonderful old dogs are "left over" in shelters because many visitors prefer a young dog. Of course, old dogs may need more care than young or younger dogs.

And it can happen that you have to visit the veterinarian more often with an old dog, and possibly higher costs will arise. This cannot be denied and should be considered when purchasing a dog, especially when chronic diseases are present or operations are necessary. But what will happen, regardless of age, is that you will be loved unconditionally! An old dog in particular will show you his gratitude all the more for the fact that you have taken him into your home and offered him a beautiful old age.

You cannot decide whether young or old? Both have advantages and disadvantages, as described. You should consider carefully which advantages of young or old are more important for you personally and which disadvantages you would rather avoid. Remember that there are millions of stray dogs worldwide who are neither very young nor very old. At least one of them will definitely fit you!

Excursus to the question: How old is my dog in human years?

The conversion that 1 dog year corresponds to about 7 human years is now considered obsolete. So, small dogs age faster as puppies than large breeds, but with increasing age, it is exactly the other way round. With large dogs, the aging process accelerates; with the smaller dogs it progresses more and more slowly. The smaller the breed, the shorter the childhood phase, but overall, smaller dogs usually have a higher life expectancy than their larger conspecifics.

In addition to the size, the weight of the dog must also be taken into account when determining his age. Other factors also have an influence on the age a dog can reach. These include, for example, a hereditary predisposition to various diseases, specific characteristics with regard to the breed of dog and the respective way of life. By the way, bitches live on average 2 to 2.5 years more than male dogs.

Veterinary Professor Jean-Louis Pouchelon of the Alfort Veterinary School (France) drew up a table in 1998 to facilitate the conversion into human years. The table "Dog years in human years" clearly shows how you can calculate the age of your dog (German picture source: www.hund-als-haustier.de).

Dog years in human years

below 15 kg   15 to 45 kg   above 45 kg

Dog years	Human years		
0,5	15	10	8
1	20	18	14
1,5	24	21	18
2	28	27	22
3	32	33	31
4	36	39	40
5	40	45	49
6	44	51	58
7	48	57	67
8	52	63	76
9	56	69	85
10	60	75	94
11	64	80	103
12	68	85	
13	72	90	
14	76	95	
15	80	100	
16	84	105	
17	88		
18	92		
19	96		
20	100		

Puppy	Adult	Senior	Old dog

Sex

This decision is probably not so easy and in many cases it is a matter of taste. Males are said to be less affectionate than females. But this is definitely not true - our Bernese Mountain Dog Merlin is the best example of this!

A few details about male dogs

With male dogs, it can happen that they show more dominance towards humans and other dogs, and, especially with other males, they like to start one or other scuffle. This usually looks worse than it actually is, and usually nothing dramatic happens - mostly it is just showing off. If this behavior becomes rampant, castration might help, and the earlier it is done, the better.

Basically, neutering should only be done if there is a medical necessity for it. In the case of Merlin, we had to have him castrated not because of any macho behavior, but for health reasons. He had a cyst on his prostate (a cancer), which caused bleeding when he urinated and was removed as a preventive measure. The castration was carried out at the same time to spare him the strain of another operation. A castration can also be helpful if a male dog leaves his individual scent at every imaginable and sometimes impossible spot by marking it, or almost goes crazy if a female dog is in heat somewhere in the neighborhood. Regardless of whether they are in heat or not, male dogs usually get along very well with female dogs. And if a "macho" dog meets a neutered male dog, there are fewer problems than when two non-neutered male dogs meet.

A few details about female dogs

If you want a female dog, be prepared to have her in heat twice a year. In some breeds this happens only once a year. It usually lasts 21 days and means that the female dog has reached sexual maturity or is entering the fertile phase of her life. Being in heat causes the female dog's behavior to change and she has to urinate more often than usual when walking. The fact that (uncastrated) male dogs show an increased interest in the female dog also makes the heat phase noticeable.The exact time of the heat period is difficult to predict, but it usually occurs for the first time between 6 and 12 months of age, and thereafter approximately every 7 months and in 4 phases. Already from the first phase, the female dog smells very tempting, and you should keep a respectful distance from non-neutered male dogs when walking. This is mainly because you don't know in which phase of the female dog's heat cycle she is, and, in addition, it is a precautionary measure to ensure that nothing "undesirable" happens.

In the first phase, the female dog excretes drops of blood from time to time. It is advisable to put on a special "protective panty" for the female dog, which you can get in specialist shops. This will prevent unsightly drops of blood from being dispersed in your home. If you are not planning to have a new generation, the female dog should be neutered. On top of that, this can greatly reduce the risk of developing mammary tumors and uterine diseases. As far as social behavior is concerned, female dogs usually get along with all male dogs, although male dogs often do not have much to say. If a female dog also gets along with other female dogs, this is the most uncomplicated stroke of luck. When two female dogs meet, one of whom does not like the other at all, trouble is much more likely to be pre-programmed than with two incompatible male dogs. Problems can sometimes occur when a dominant female dog meets a neutered male dog, because they cannot "match" them.

Breed

As far as this topic is concerned, you should not make your choice on the basis of a more or less attractive appearance. It is not important whether a dog is "beautiful." Much more important is whether you and the dog are a good match - especially with regard to his attributes and character. Of course, there are subjectively beautiful pedigree dogs, but unfortunately it is often the case with these in particular that much more importance is attached to their outward appearance and breeding than to all other characteristics. Among other things, this development favors the spread of hereditary diseases or predisposition to diseases that are typical for some breeds. With increasing age, these include, for example, problems with the bones, especially with the hip joints, tumor formation and subsequent cancer, blindness or deafness.

In general, it is very worrying that dog breeding often achieves bad physical results, such as dogs that have been bred short-legged from birth and can hardly walk, have trouble breathing due to their flat noses or are more prone to ear, eye and skin infections due to a wrinkled "beautiful" face. In addition, such breedings can produce dogs with not impeccable character, which is equally questionable.

Therefore, I would like to point out the numerous types of mixed breeds, which combine many a great trait and character of two (or more) breeds. Mixed breeds are also great companions in life, sport partners and lovable family members. Should you choose a mixed breed, you will usually have a truly unique dog. In addition, it is said that mixed breeds are often healthier and sometimes even smarter - so they are actually the better choice. As with any dog, (hereditary) diseases can also occur in mixed breeds, which in individual cases are promoted by unfavorable matings. In general, however, there is nothing to be said against choosing mixed breeds.

Size

Basically, a dog should fit your individual living conditions and he should be able to move around – no matter what size he is – in your apartment or house. But he doesn't have to run a race inside, because you walk him or take him to a dog exercise area. It should be clear that a child cannot go for a walk with a St.

Bernard dog, which may weigh twice as much as the child does. In such a case, a smaller dog would probably be more sensible. The same applies if you go for a walk with a large uneducated dog, who may also react quite impulsively and like to put your assertiveness and physical strength to the test. Nevertheless, small dogs are often much more lively, spirited, cheeky and exhausting than large dogs.

Big dogs eat more than small ones in any case - but sometimes the small ones want only the most expensive food and so the costs balance each other out. And, of course, big dogs need more space (in the car or at home in the room or on the couch) - in contrast, small dogs can often be real nuisances. In any case, one should not necessarily be confused by the size of a dog, and, for example, not automatically assume that small dogs mean little work for you and large dogs mean a lot of work.

Origin

No matter what you decide, whether puppy or adult dog, pedigree or crossbreed: look for your dog in the animal shelters in your area and visit the mediation sites of serious animal protection associations on the internet. You do not necessarily have to go to a breeder to find a specific dog or breed. For almost every breed there is now a corresponding "breed X in distress" club, where you might find your future roommate. But please beware of buying dogs from so-called "breeders" who offer purebred puppies at lowest prices. These puppies usually come from Eastern Europe and from mass breeding, where the bitches suffer greatly. The puppies - often barely 8 weeks old - are separated from their mothers, exposed to long car journeys in inadequate accommodation and then usually presented in parking lots or sometimes even sold directly from the trunk. In some cases, the puppies are even advertised via the internet. Please never buy such a puppy! In general, you should never buy a puppy from a "breeder" who can't show you the parents and at least the mother of the puppy and their accommodation.

In animal shelters and animal protection societies, you can look around in peace, and, if you are interested, you can get to know a dog better - which is best during several walks together. In addition, you will receive useful information about the dog's past history, as well as his good and bad sides - and you will certainly always be given honest advice! After all, it is never in the interest of an animal shelter if a mediation breaks down due to misinformation and the dog ends up at the shelter again. However, you should be prepared for the fact that you will be asked about your personal life situation and they will possibly want to have a look at your apartment or house. Please do not react angrily or negatively in such a case. This is all for the good of the dog. After all, the dog should find a home in which he can live happily together with you!

If you want to give a dog from the shelter a new home and there is - for whatever reason - an unsolvable problem, every serious shelter will take the dog back. If you are interested in a mongrel, you could consider another search variant. In Germany, for example, dogs from almost the whole world are placed, because animal misery is very big everywhere. Therefore, foreign animal welfare activists are dependent on the mediation of dogs also to Germany. Respectable foreign associations cooperate very closely with German animal welfare societies and have several additional foster homes for dogs in Germany. In Germany, as an interested party in a foreign dog, you will be advised just as extensively and informed about country-specific risks of illness, and within the framework of the mediation, there is the so-called protection contract.

However, do not make the mistake of ordering a foreign dog on the internet and picking up the dog at an airport yourself. You do not know this dog at all, you do not get any information about him and you do not get a protection contract. This means that you are on your own in the case of any problems and there are no contact persons in your area to whom you can turn. If something goes wrong in such a case, you cannot simply put the dog into a transport box and send him back to the place of dispatch.

Accommodation

Please be aware that a dog by nature does not live on his own. The most important thing in the life of a family dog is his place in "his" pack. Therefore, a dog should not be chained, put in a kennel or locked away in a cage in front of the house or somewhere in the garden (no matter if it is in the garden, on the terrace, on the balcony or even inside the house). A family dog should be allowed access to the house or his family at any time and thus be able to contact his "pack."

Ideally, the dog should be allowed to stay where his family is, i.e., usually in the apartment or house. Of course, there are dogs who like to lie around outside in the garden, but they too want to go back to their humans at some point. In the apartment or house, the dog will choose his own preferred place, unless you show him where you want him to go - otherwise he is guaranteed to find a place for himself that he may not be entitled to (for example, your bed or couch). A tip for the case that your dog likes to lie on a higher level and prefers to use the couch for this: maybe you can find an old TV armchair, which you can equip with a blanket and then leave it to your dog.

Dogs and other (domestic) animals

You would like to take in a dog and already have other animals in your house? This should not be a headache for you, because, in the end, it is up to you, your patience and your assertiveness and not so much up to the dog, for the living together to go well. Maybe, due to the different body language, some misunderstandings can arise, but living together can still be harmonious. It is very possible to teach a dog that the animals that belong to the family are absolutely taboo for him - even if the dog is actually a hunter.

Of course, a rabbit, guinea pig, cat or bird are and remain a possible prey of the dog. Therefore, especially in the phase of getting to know each other, one should not leave the animals completely alone and unattended, until there is little doubt that your dog will really leave the other animal housemates alone.

After all, you are not only responsible for the dog, but also for your other pets. And this responsibility continues when you go for a walk in nature, because every dog has a more or less trained hunting instinct and he will take advantage of the moment if you are distracted for a second or even let him run free. If you do not have a reliable grip on the dog, he will run away and devote himself to hunting mice, birds, rabbits, hares, deer or wild boars. Please make sure that this does not happen, and do not endanger the lives of other animals (or your dog if he runs away and gets into traffic) with brief inattention.

CHAPTER 4: Tips for your life with a dog

In order for you and your dog to have a successful start for a future together, a little planning is necessary before your new roommate moves in. This is not only about the location of the dog basket or the choice of toys, but also about the basics of how humans and animals live together.

What a family dog needs to be happy

Family dogs need:

- a stable family with a fixed (subordinate) place in the ranking
- clear rules and consistent people who do not say yes today and no tomorrow
- People with time, empathy, good nerves and healthy minds
- extensive movement (not only on a leash, but also "free" time) with alternative and therefore varied routes for the walk
- mental stimulation and challenges, for example by doing search games or by learning some tricks
- a healthy diet which is adapted to the age of the dog
- conspecifics to play and romp around with
- people with whom they are allowed to be dogs and are not humanized
- people who have fun when their dog now and again happily rolls around in the mud
- time for games and strokes
- a quiet place and undisturbed sleep
- someone who never tugs at them, yells at them for no reason or uses violence against them

Basic preparations

- Choose a name (there are many portals on the internet with ideas for the name of your dog).
- Take out dog liability insurance (very important in case you are living in a rented house or if something happens in traffic).
- Carry out dog tax registration at your place of residence.
- Prepare the bed(s) for the dog.

- Define those areas in the house or apartment where the dog is not allowed to go (and secure them, for example, with a door grille).
- If there is a garden, it should be made "escape-proof," but please note: puppies can squeeze through tiny gaps and also under the fence!
- Look for a dog school or a group of puppies and go there without a dog to get first impressions.
- Read puppy education books.
- Discuss with the family and determine what the dog is allowed to do and what he is not allowed to do.

Initial equipment

You should get the most important items of the following initial equipment before the puppy/dog moves in with you, because once he is in your home, for some time, there will be no opportunity for extended shopping.

Dog harness or dog collar

Especially for a puppy, a dog harness is definitely better suited than a dog collar. The puppy will very often pull on the leash during the education phase for different reasons, and every jerk puts equal strain on his neck and spine. And, of course, it can also happen that the puppy slips out of the collar and can then often be caught again only with difficulty. This can lead to dicey situations, or your dog runs so far away that you can no longer find him. With a properly secured harness, such a thing cannot happen at all. When buying a dog harness, you should pay attention to the following points. The material should be adapted to the dog's fur, which means, for example, long hair should not get tangled up in the harness. Good padding of the harness contributes to a comfortable fit. With puppies, it is also very important that the harness can still "grow" with the puppy and does not cut into him. If the dog has pain when wearing the harness, you and your dog will not enjoy walks together.

Leading leash, running and rolling leash

The leading leash should be 1.5 or 2 m long, a running leash 5 m or longer. By the way, running leashes are also called towing, search or field leashes. With a running leash, the puppy has more freedom of movement when walking outside the town or city and more opportunities to go on a (controlled) tour of discovery. On paths where there are many pedestrians, cyclists or joggers, the running leash is more of a hindrance. For the time being, it is better to use only a so-called leading leash when walking with your puppy. This is also very suitable for the education of your dog. With the leading leash, you can best influence the puppy. A rolling leash (often called a flexi-leash) is not suitable for training, even if it seems very practical. There is a very large selection of leading leash lines and one can be quickly tempted by somewhat unusual variations. Please make sure that the width, length and weight of the leash fits your puppy! And you should know that puppies love to nibble on things. Because they don't stop at a leash, a reserve leash would be a good idea.

With regard to rolling leashes, I would like to point out that handling them can be dangerous for your dog and yourself. For example, your dog can injure himself if the leash is attached to his collar and he suddenly wants to chase a cat that suddenly appears. He starts at first unhindered and is stopped very rudely when the leash is fully unrolled, and, in combination with his collar, he can even be severely choked.

Smaller dogs may also be very rudely catapulted back in such a situation. For this reason, a leash should always be used in combination with a chest harness. In addition, it is very important that you are not distracted when using a leash, but always keep a close eye on your dog and the surroundings. You too can get painful injuries if you reach for the rolling leash of your dog who is suddenly running away, or if you  accidentally touch the leash with your fingers. This can lead to burns, abrasions and sometimes very deep cuts on your fingers and/or hand.

Until Merlin went through puberty and became calmer, we always used a chest harness in combination with a rolling leash when we went for a walk, especially outside the city. There were never any injuries to him or to us, because we were watching him closely and because we could always stop a sudden start immediately.

Food

Here it is very important that you inquire about which food the dog/puppy has received so far. He should continue to get this food from you, so that there is no unpleasant surprise with vomiting or diarrhea right at the beginning. Both can be caused by a too quick food change. If you know what food your dog has been fed so far, then get enough of it so that you have it available in the first 2 to 3 weeks. It is best to have a feeding plan that you can stick to in the first days or weeks. For a puppy in particular, it is already a big change to be torn out of his familiar environment and separated from his family. Therefore, you should not expect him to change his food immediately. Even if you have already decided on a different food or a different feeding method for later, wait a little longer until your dog has settled in with you.

When you choose your dog's food, please remember that it should be according to his age. This means that a puppy should not be given food for an adult dog, as the nutritional content and especially the needs of the dog are completely different. With dry food, it can also happen that the chunks are too hard for a puppy's milk teeth. If you want to change the food you are currently using to a different food, always do this gradually. This means that every day you add a few grams of the new food and leave out these few grams of the previous food. Do this until the food ration consists only of the new food. This slow change will prevent your dog from getting diarrhoea or other side effects such as vomiting.

Keep an eye on your dog during the changeover and check for skin rashes, for example. If this is the case, you should stop feeding the new food. We have changed Merlin's food in puppyhood, as a young dog, as an adult and most recently at the beginning of his senior phase and it has always worked very well. Unfortunately, because he often had skin rashes on his belly until he was 5 years old, we decided on a somewhat more expensive food at that time, but it paid off. The rashes disappeared, Merlin's coat became shinier and he generally felt better due to the higher quality ingredients.

By the way, you should expect your dog to get flatulence, for example, when changing his food or feeding a new type of treat. This can be very smelly and you should consider this when you have visitors at home and your dog is lying with stomach turbulence right under the table where you are sitting with your guests. This unexpected odor nuisance can, of course, also occur during a visit to a restaurant where you have your dog with you. In this case it is best to take your dog out into the fresh air for a short time, perhaps he will then do some big business that has caused the flatulence.

Feeding bowl and water bowl

Just like the bed for your new family member, the food and water bowl also require your personal taste, because these two bowls will be part of your interior design, and, in the best case, you will see them every day for the next few years. Apart from an attractive design, there are a few more important things you should consider so that your dog can use the bowls properly and safely. The food and water bowls should be easy to clean so that a certain level of hygiene can always be maintained. Both bowls should be slightly larger than the head size of the adult dog, so that you do not have to do a basic cleaning at the feeding place after each meal. If you wish, you can also place a wipeable and non-slip pad under the bowls. Not only the underlay but also the bowls themselves should be non-slip. There are bowls with rubber edges or rubber studs. This prevents them from slipping away during eating or drinking and the puppy pushing the bowl through your apartment or house. Furthermore, if the dog moves the bowl roughly, neither the food nor the water should be tipped out. Remember also that the bowls should be sturdy. Dogs rarely handle the bowls with care.

Toys

Just like small children, little puppies are very playful and curious and want to explore the world. There are many different toys that can keep the little ones on their toes. Since you certainly do not know at the beginning what your puppy likes to play with, offer him different toys. However, please always make sure that you buy toys that are subject to appropriate certifications. For example, they should not contain any small parts that could be swallowed and they should not contain any harmful substances. Never give your dog old shoes or socks to play with, as he cannot distinguish between old and new and will fetch what he likes from his own easily available supply. The classic among dog toys is, of course, the ball. It rolls and bounces, and the puppy can run after it. If the ball has nubs on it, the dog can hold it in his mouth and it stimulates the gums. Make sure that the ball is neither too small nor too big for the puppy, otherwise the desire to play with the ball can disappear very quickly. Latex chewing toys with and without squeaking prove to be just as popular. However, there are dogs that are afraid of squeaking. On top of that, you should consider whether you can stand the constant or frequent squeaking while your dog is playing.

Other chewing toys, which are very helpful especially during tooth replacement, are chewing wedges or chewing knots. In many cases, soft toys are also very popular with dogs. As mentioned before, one should make sure that they do not contain any parts that can be easily swallowed (e.g., button eyes). It can happen that the puppy disassembles the soft toy into its individual parts and eats the insides of the soft toy, which is definitely not recommended for consumption. Highly recommended are products with thinking games, in which the dog is encouraged to think for himself how to get treats. This will stimulate the puppy's intelligence, but he should not be overexerted. After all, brainwork is very strenuous for dogs, even if we don't see it at first glance. 5 to 10 minutes is completely sufficient for a puppy! Just as strenuous are search games, by the way, in which you distribute treats in the garden or on a lawn and let him "sniff" them.

Dog bed or dog box for rest periods

A puppy spends up to 22 hours a day sleeping; an adult dog snoozes or sleeps an average of 14 to 20 hours. In order to ensure that the dog really has his peace and quiet during this time, you should create a protected or at least a quiet retreat and assign him a fixed place there. This is where you place a dog bed or a dog box for him. An important factor when making this purchase is the size of the bed or box.

A rule of thumb for the right size is that the puppy should be able to stretch out all four legs when lying down. However, the bed or box should not be too big, because otherwise the puppy feels lost in it. By the way, dog beds with a surrounding edge are very popular with four-legged

friends because they can snuggle in comfortably and the edge gives them a feeling of protection. Please also remember that the puppy will nibble on different things, and this can include his own sleeping place. Therefore, you should choose a smaller, more robust version at the beginning and only later change to a larger dog bed, which offers enough space for your adult dog. A dog box has an additional benefit - you can also use it for transport in a car. Of course, you have to choose a version that fits in your car and also offers enough space for your dog. If you don't have a dog box in your car, you should at least make sure that there is a well-fixed separating net, or, even better, a stable separating grille between the passenger compartment and the boot. This measure protects your dog and you in case you have to brake suddenly. If your car has a high loading sill, it is advisable for dogs that are still growing, as well as for older dogs, to purchase a dog ramp. With this, you can let the dog get in and out of the car without harming his joints. If a dog is used to the ramp from a young age, then he will also use it gladly in old age. We bought such a ramp for our Bernese Mountain Dog puppy Merlin and he has always enjoyed using it. This way, his joints have been spared, he is still top fit and has no joint problems whatsoever.

Door or playpen

If you live in a house, you can use a grille to secure any open stairs (down to the cellar or up to the first floor). A growing puppy or dog should preferably not climb stairs yet, so it is good to prevent him from doing so. In addition, the grille is very suitable for limiting the puppy's range of movement for a short time - for example, if the parcel carrier rings or you have a guest and you don't want the puppy to rush at the visitor.

Dog excrement bag

An important issue, which should be self-evident for a dog owner, is the removal of the feces of the new family member. For this there are dog excrement bags - special plastic bags, which in Germany are provided free of charge in many cities along the walking paths. As an alternative to a plastic excrement bag, you can equip yourself with a more environmentally friendly version, which is made of corn starch and is biodegradable. For easy stowage and problem-free carrying of these helpful bags, there are special bag holders available in specialist shops, which you can easily attach to the leash, your trouser belt or a bag. We always have a stock of excrement bags in the car, so that we can equip ourselves from the beginning of the walk, just in case. Tip: We always take at least two dog excrement bags with us when we go for a walk, just in case Merlin does more than one big business during the walk. But please don't throw the leftovers collected in the dog excrement bag just anywhere if you don't find a trash can right away! Normally there is always a trash can somewhere on public roads and in parking lots - you just have to take the leftover dog excrement a few steps to the next trash can. A properly disposed dog excrement bag prevents you from upsetting your fellow citizens and guarantees that nature is protected!

Facts worth knowing about a dog

Puppies are born blind and deaf: Newborn dogs take quite a while before they can see. They don't open their eyes until 10 to 15 days after birth, and they can't see clearly until they are about a month old. Speaking of vision: Dogs recognize colors, and their color vision is similar to that of humans who suffer from red-green vision deficiency. Dogs cannot perceive red colors, but they can perceive yellow, green, turquoise, blue and violet. The sense of hearing of a puppy develops from the 12th day and the complete hearing a dog baby acquires at the age of approximately 4 to 6 weeks. By the way, a dog can move its ears independently and in a large radius. A total of 17 muscles are responsible for this great mobility. This allows it to orient each ear appropriately to pick up the sound waves from a sound source. This allows the dog to hear your voice no matter what direction it comes from.

Dogs hear wider frequency ranges: Humans can perceive sound frequencies from about 20 hertz upward. In everyday life, we are confronted with sounds in a range of about 64 to 2,000 Hz. Dogs and humans perceive these about equally well. 20,000 Hz is the maximum pitch that a human with good hearing can perceive, but only very faintly. A dog can perceive up to 65,000 Hz, depending on the breed. Dogs therefore have two decisive advantages over us humans: First, they hear more accurately where a sound is coming from and they can direct their ear to the sound source. Secondly, they hear a much wider frequency range and thus also sounds that we humans cannot perceive at all.

Puppies first get 28 milk teeth: only after that the permanent dentition develops from 42 teeth, 10 more than we humans have. The milk teeth usually emerge between the third and sixth week of life and are evenly distributed between the upper jaw and the lower jaw at 5 to 6 weeks. Thus, there are six molars on the top and bottom, two canines, and six incisors. Between the 4th and 7th month of life, the milk dentition changes to the permanent dentition, often a little earlier in large dogs than in small ones. During the change of teeth you should not play tug games, they can cause pain to the dog. Rather give him chewing products or toys to nibble on, it massages his gums at the same time. An adult dog has two canines, twelve molars and six incisors in the upper jaw. In the lower jaw of the quadruped are also two canines and six incisors, but 14 molars, that is, two molars more than above. Beware of very hard chewing products such as deer antler and coffee root, these can lead to tooth chipping, which will not only cause pain, but in the worst case, the loss of the tooth. Alternatively, you can give your dog a Torgas root to nibble on.

Puppies sleep almost all day: they snooze up to 22 hours a day and this is also the case with old and sick dogs. Lack of sleep can cause serious health problems for dogs. Only dogs that sleep enough can develop healthily and normally. So give your dog his daily sleep time and help him to rest. This can be done very well with a dog bed, placed in a quiet place, where your dog feels safe. Like humans, dogs have two sleep phases: A deep sleep phase and a light sleep phase. In the deep sleep phase, your dog dreams and processes what he has experienced before. Adult dogs sleep 14 to 20 hours per day - allow your dog the daily minimum of sleep.

Dogs have a higher body temperature: it is between 37.5 and 39 degrees Celsius in a healthy animal. In humans, the normal body temperature is between 36.5 and 37.4 degrees Celsius. If a dog's temperature is only slightly and briefly elevated, nothing needs to be done. However, if the body temperature rises above 41 degrees, then a veterinarian should be consulted. In this case, there may be an acute danger to the dog. You can find more information about fever and measuring fever in chapter 7. under "Diseases".

Dogs sweat via their tongues: they have only a few sweat glands on their pads and under their paws and therefore cool themselves via their tongues: If it gets too hot for them, they start panting. The breathing rate can increase up to ten times the normal rate. Since panting also evaporates a lot of moisture, it is enormously important that the dog drinks a lot of water. Please never leave your dog alone in the car when the outside temperature is above 20 degrees Celsius, in the worst case it can suffer from heat stroke or circulatory collapse!

The dog's nose is the most important sensory organ: dogs have up to 220 million olfactory cells, humans only 5 million. Thus, dogs have at least 40 times more olfactory cells than we do and they can therefore smell up to 1 million times better. The longer a dog's snout, the larger the nasal conchae and the better the sense of smell, which dogs use to find their way around the environment and detect odors even from great distances. Dogs' noses also serve to humidify, warm and, most importantly, purify the air they breathe. With the help of their sense of smell, dogs can even detect human diseases such as cancer. By the way, dogs don't like the smell of citrus, vinegar, ammonia and hot peppers at all, so for your dog's sake, keep these scents away from him.

Dog saliva contains antibacterial components: Researchers at the University of Bern found that dog saliva contains a substance called lysozyme. This is effective against some bacteria such as streptococci and staphylococci. Dog saliva also contains immunoglobolins (antibodies), which also play an important role in the defence system of humans. As a rule, it is not a problem if your dog licks your hands, arms or legs. A slobbery dog kiss on the cheek or chin is also harmless. However, you should not let your dog lick your face (especially your eyes, nose and mouth) or at least wash yourself immediately afterwards.

CHAPTER 5: Your dog moves in

Tips for day one

A fantastic time awaits you! Start living together in peace and quiet and take the time to get to know each other - a few days' holiday is perfect for this. While you just expand your existing life, the whole world changes for your dog. You will be amazed how quickly your four-legged friend will find his place at your side! In the following, I mainly describe the moving-in procedure for a puppy, but there are also various tips for future living together with an older dog.

Making it easier for your dog to move in

Just a moment ago, he was lying next to his siblings and his mother under the heat lamp in the cuddly litter box, now suddenly everything is new and different. To make the journey to your home as free of fear and stress as possible, you can calm the puppy with pheromones.

These are odorous substances which are produced by bitches about three to five days after the birth of the puppies in the suckling box. These substances not only have a calming effect on puppies, but also on older dogs. When you pick up your puppy, it's best to take an old bath towel with you and place the puppy on it.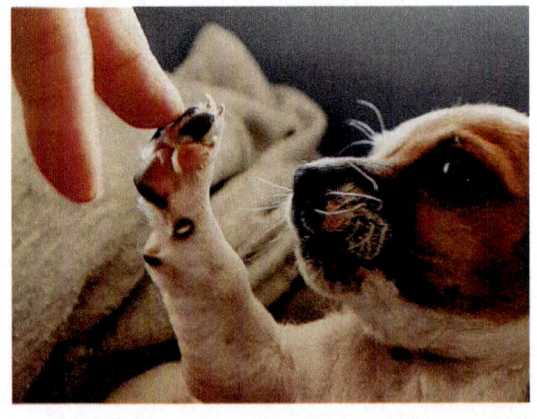
Ideally, the dog should not be put in a transport box, but rather someone should take him on his lap and hold him. The bath towel can prevent the excited puppy from urinating uncontrollably and it also helps in the event of vomiting.

Not only the cutting of the cord from his mother and the separation from his brothers and sisters is stressful for your puppy, in addition, at your home, everything smells different, everything sounds different and everything looks different. Your dog has to get used to a completely new environment with new stimuli and new "pack members" and needs your help. Offer him your proximity and do not leave him alone anywhere, especially in the first few nights. He needs rest, your patience and many strokes, so that he feels safe and secure.

A relaxed yet safe atmosphere

Even before he moves in, you should make your apartment or house and garden puppy-proof and escape-proof. Protect your curious roommate from electric cables, plants and steep stairs, and take precautions to keep the expensive carpets safe.

Curiosity often drives a puppy into situations that can become dangerous for him. Put dangers such as medication, cleaning agents, detergents or cigarettes away just as safely as chocolate - which, like all sweets, can become life-threatening for dogs! Here, I would also like to point out that you should never leave your dog (just like any freely moving pet) alone in a room with a candle burning (keyword: Advent wreath or Christmas tree). With a larger dog, such as our Bernese Mountain Dog, it can also happen that he knocks something over by wagging his tail when passing a low chest of drawers or a coffee table - this can be a candle as well as a vase or a glass, etc. Therefore check your home if all rooms accessible to the dog are dog-safe. The same applies if you visit someone with your dog.

The lower the risk for the dog and your household goods, the more relaxed you can be about your protégé. During the first few nights in particular, the puppy will miss his cuddly pack. It is good for him if his dog bed is placed near you, where he can hear your breath and feel your presence. Your caressing hand relieves his nightmares and you can react quickly when the fullness of his bladder is pressing. By the way: There's nothing wrong with letting the puppy sleep in your bed for the first few days. Don't worry, you can teach him later that he's not allowed to sleep in bed, but only in the space allocated to him or in his dog bed.

Grant the new roommate a settling-in period

In the rest lies the power and in the acclimatisation period both you and your dog will need a lot of energy. Your new roommate is entering a world full of exciting impressions, new rules and daily routines - it is therefore good to know that dogs are true masters of adaptation. How long it takes your dog to get used to the new environment depends on many factors: Older dogs, for example, usually manage it more easily than a puppy. The better the dog's characteristics suit you, the quicker it will adapt to its new home - in this respect, the animal is no different from people. If the chemistry between you and the animal is right, a familiarisation period of about two weeks is a good guideline. Of course, every dog has its own character and it can take longer or shorter.

And no matter how tempting it may be, please spare the puppy visits from family members, friends or acquaintances in the first few days and give the dog a breather after the exciting change of residence. Take the time to get to know each other and try to find a common rhythm. Only when the dog has become accustomed to you as a caregiver can others welcome the new family member. Help your dog to settle in with a quiet environment, walks together, cosy cuddles on the sofa and exuberant games.

Also use the time to get your four-legged partner used to the coat, ear and claw care at an early stage. Brush him regularly, take a quick look at his ears every now and then and take his paws in your hand for a test – all this is a good preparation for him to do this later without any resistance (when you do the grooming or someone else does it). For all procedures that are only carried out unwillingly, calm but specific words and little treats are the right choice.

Dog run and and regular time-out

A puppy needs to relieve himself every two hours or so, but always immediately after sleeping, eating, drinking and playing. You should try to anticipate his timing and take him outside regularly before it is too late. This should help him to become housebroken relatively quickly. A puppy needs exercise and wants to explore the environment – but all in moderation. As soon as he gets tired, you should make your way home. Puppies need regular sleep breaks and take 30 up to 60 minutes naps several times a day. With a soft dog pillow or a cuddly dog bed you can sweeten his time out and at the same time assign him a fixed place.

Duration of the walk

Take for a puppy as a rule of thumb: 5 minutes per month of life - preferably often, but never too long! A puppy shouldn't take long walks because he is in the middle of growth, his bones are soft and not so resilient, and his joints are not yet closed. Conversely, as your dog gets older, you should reduce the number of walks and the time per walk if you notice that your dog tires more quickly than before, for example, if after a certain distance he slows down or pants more strongly.

Pay attention and always keep an eye on your dog

Please also take it to heart to leave your mobile phone plugged in at home when walking your dog and not to make phone calls or send messages on the side. If you always keep an eye on your dog and his actions, you can react immediately if he tries to eat something forbidden or wants to go off somewhere. To prevent your dog from picking up something edible or to get your dog to spit out the "something" picked up in his mouth, it is best to use a specific command such as „Yuck". Use this word from an early age when he finds something and wants to eat it. You never know what he has just caught and wants to swallow. An additional solution is that you offer your dog a treat to swap. When your dog spits out its "prey", it will receive the treat in return.

In the dark, it will be even more difficult to see what your dog has discovered along the way. So as soon as your dog starts sniffing more intensively somewhere, there is something interesting there that he might want to grab and eat. Speaking of sniffing: dogs have many times the number of olfactory cells that a human has. For comparison: humans have about 5 million olfactory cells, dachshunds about 125 million and German shepherds even about 220 million. So if you take your dog for a walk in the dark, a flashlight or the flashlight function of your mobile phone is helpful to see what your dog is sniffing or eating.

If you are in a rural area and you let your dog run free there, you should also always watch him. After all, he could suddenly run away at any time, for example, because he wants to chase another animal. In urban areas, on the other hand, your dog can also endanger himself and others by carelessly running away, for example, when he crosses a cycle path or runs across the road.

What could also happen: Your dog discovers a dead animal or a place where one has been and then starts to roll on the animal or on this place. He does this, for example, to take on the smell for camouflage and thus cover up his own, to show other dogs that he has killed a prey or to mark something potentially edible as his property. We always interrupted Merlin's rolling and immediately fetched him to us because we thought it was disgusting.

Incidentally, fetching him is also highly recommended if you are walking your dog along a field where the farmer has emptied fresh manure. It happened to us once with Merlin (and then never again) that he rolled in such a field. We had to wash him several times at home with dog shampoo to neutralise the very intense smell. I will go into more detail about washing in the chapter "Coat care".

New pack, new rules

From the first moment on you should teach the puppy the new house rules, consistently ignore unwanted behavior and reward good behavior with immediate praise or treats. In order to create a good bond, you should show him from the very beginning that it is worth being near you, that he can trust you and that he can orientate himself to you. The puppy learns this when fighting over toys, cuddling, brushing or feeding.

The curriculum should also include teaching respect and distance. You decide when to play or cuddle, when the dog may approach and when not. This sounds strict, but is natural and important for the puppy in the socialization phase that is now taking place, so that he can get to know you and his new pack better.

There are rules not only for your four-legged friend, but also for all two-legged friends living in the same household. In a certain situation, commands should only be given by one person and not simultaneously or alternately by two people. If there are children in the house, they have to learn how to deal with the new roommate as well, and follow rules. This includes, without exception, leaving the dog alone when drinking and eating.

Here I would like to point out an exercise that we did several times with Merlin in puppyhood. It is about a dog possibly defending his toy, his chew bone or his food and growling at you or other people while doing so. This is a way of defending resources and a quite understandable behavior, because, after all, we humans also want to hold onto those things that are important to us or that satisfy our needs. And so does your dog. If the growl is followed by aggressive behavior such as snapping or even biting, you should show your dog that resource defense is not necessary and that he can trust you if you approach him, for example, while he is nibbling on his chewing bone. We have practiced this regularly with Merlin as a preventive measure by rewarding him with a special treat if he let us have his filled food bowl, his chewing bone or toy. Afterwards, he got the food, bone or toy back, and so he learned that there was no reason to defend anything. Regarding his food, you can feed it directly from your hand over a period of time to show him that you are sharing the food with him and not taking it away.

Back to your children: if they are big enough to run around and you can already explain something to them, then tell them that they must not pull or pinch any part of the dog's body (ears, tail, flews, legs etc.) because it is uncomfortable and because it hurts. After all, nobody likes it if you pull or pinch them - certainly not your offspring. If your children are still too small for explanations, never leave them alone with the dog. According to the motto, "Trust is good, control is better."

In general, I recommend never to leave small children alone with a dog, even if your dog is used to this and there has never been a negative event. You never know what your own or a visiting child will do with the dog during the unobserved time. At this point I would like to tell you a short story from my own experience: My sister and I as children once visited a farm, where there was a dachshund and a German Wirehair („Deutsch Drahthaar") hunting dog. The dachshund was locked away during our visit because it was considered to be biting. The Deutsch Drahthaar lay outside in the meadow where my sister and I played with the children from the farm. While jumping around, my sister unintentionally bumped into the dog and he jumped up and bit her in the face.

This did not happen out of malice, but only because the sleeping dog was rudely awakened and my sister had probably hurt it with the push. The bite to the face left no serious injury or scarring, thank God, but the event shows that care should always be taken when a dog is present.

Incidentally, this incident, which was her fault, meant that my sister was later not afraid of dogs, quite the contrary. As soon as her life situation allowed it, she got her own dog and this was a very friendly female Rottweiler. Later a Bernese Mountain Dog (the mother of our Merlin) followed and today a female Rottweiler lives with her again.

Also remember that you and your children should allow the dog to have undisturbed breaks. This is especially true when the dog is retiring to sleep. If you send him to his place and want him to stay there, your children should not approach the dog, touch him or lure him away from there. Also, make sure that your children do not play or jump around near the sleeping dog. As mentioned before his could frighten him and make him snap at the child as a reflex.

Don't forget to pay attention to the socialization with other dogs at an early stage. For example, you can visit a puppy class and - if available - take a look at the local dog playground from time to time. Dogs are very sociable creatures and enjoy playing with their conspecifics. It means nothing bad if your puppy scraps with other dogs and sometimes maybe squeals in fright. Through these quarrels among conspecifics he can gain experience in dealing with others and he also learns when there are limits to his temperament.

If something goes wrong

If the start of life as a dog owner should be a bit bumpy, it is first of all necessary to keep calm and not to despair. The dog does not eat or deflates inside the house? That can be due to excitement or due to the food. Find out which food the dog was used to and continue feeding him the same (for the time being). Is your dog a puppy? Find out what he likes.

After all, humans do not like all foods equally. To avoid that the dog deflates inside your apartment or house you should observe him, because this is the only way to avoid missing the decisive moment when it "pinches" him. For this reason, walk him regularly and often enough. With a puppy, you should go out into the fresh air every 2 hours, and, yes, this also applies at night! Puppies need a little longer to get the "business" under control. They usually get restless when they have to "do their business". Some then run back and forth, others sniff the ground or go round and round. At the latest then it is high time to get out. By the way, puppies usually have to do their business after sleeping, eating and playing.

It is important that you do not punish the puppy if a "mishap" has happened once. If he shows you in time that he wants to do his business, for example because he sits down at the door, praise him and go outside with him immediately. Behavior that you reward will also be shown in the future.

In small steps to the unbeatable team

There is no standardized all-round program that solves all problems that may arise. But after a few days of living together, there should at least be a foundation on which you can build. It consists at best of trust, respect, consistency and understanding of your new friend's natural needs. Once this general foundation is in place, you  will soon be as enthusiastic about your new roommate as he is about you!

CHAPTER 6: Education and behavior

Anyone who is concerned with the nature of a dog should know that dogs love clear and consistently implemented guidelines. These give him the security he needs to build a bond with his "pack". As a dog owner, this will help you in your training and at the same time your consistency will prove to be valuable for his well-being.

Dog education begins from the minute the quadruped enters his new home. At this time, you should definitely show understanding for the insecurity of the animal and respect his fears, but still teach him consistently the rules of the new pack. Of course, in dog training, harmony should always prevail. Nevertheless, it is not to be overlooked that one must show the dog boundaries, which does not always proceed harmoniously. If you are always just nice as a mistress or master, you will not be taken seriously in conflict situations.

Dog owners must therefore consistently make it clear to the dog what he is allowed and what he is not allowed to do - even if the dog sometimes doesn't like it. However, a consistent education never justifies the use of violence. If you use violence in your education, then the obedient behavior is based on fear of you and your violence. Such education and forcing the acceptance of a command is an absolute no-go.

It's better to test the effect of your voice and especially its sound. At this point the saying "The sound makes the music" also fits very well. In any case, you will be surprised how powerful your voice can be when you are educating. Your dog not only hears what you say very well (even when you speak softly), he also feels the vibrations and small nuances in your voice - and he can "read between the lines" very well. You can be sure that only hearing your voice he knows if his current behavior is ok or not. In the broadest sense, the education of a dog also includes learning tricks and solving tasks. This is a good way to keep your dog occupied and entertained. At the same time, you will certainly enjoy it just as much if your dog can solve a special task!

How many rules should be established?

There should be certain rules and guidelines for a functional coexistence between you and your dog. After all, two- and four-legged friends want to get along well and without major conflicts in their shared home. For example, you should show your dog as early as possible which areas of the apartment/house he has no business in and which behavior patterns are not accepted. With regard to the number of rules, however, it is important to find a healthy middle ground. Too many rules can be so overwhelming that the dog switches off and no longer wants to cooperate. On the other hand, your dog should not be allowed to do everything he wants - in this case he will not accept you as pack leader. There are rules that must be trained and these are definitely safety related. For example, a dog cannot judge road traffic and must therefore obey commands to ensure that he is not involved in an accident. In addition, your dog needs to learn how to behave in large crowds and towards other dogs of the same species.

Dog training according to age

In order for education to be successful, one must always consider the age of the dog. Puppies are usually very playful and one can make use of the play instinct perfectly to teach the dog something. However, the learning and exercise phases should be rather short, so that the dog does not lose attention and the desire to learn. Accept possibly initial growling or even small frictions - these are a result of the natural new division of ranking. During puberty, dogs are often unfocused, so you have to be patient and consistent during this phase. Adult dogs, on the other hand, already have their own personality and have learned certain rules, which may look different from the ones you want. Therefore it is important that you know your four-legged friend well and that you are as sensitive as possible to his nature during his upbringing. Experienced and intelligent dogs are open to new challenges and experiences. Nevertheless, you should not ignore their individual limits and preferences, but respect them.

Consequence is the be-all and end-all

Of course, it is sometimes difficult to be consistent in education. But once rules have been established, your dog will only accept them if you show consistency and show him that you mean business. For example, if you forbid begging at the table ten times and then make an exception the eleventh time, conflicts are inevitable. In this case, the dog will test how often he can get his way. With some dogs, it is particularly important to show absolute consistency. In the case of young dogs, they are further unsettled by inconsistent behavior on the part of their owners. In the long run this can lead to anxiety and, at worst, aggression. Especially with dominant dogs, an education with clear guidelines is essential and very important, because only then can you take on the role of pack leader and keep it in every situation.

Basic commands

Basic obedience should include simple commands such as "Sit", "Lie down" and "Fie" for momentary unwanted actions, and "Off" for all those behaviors that are never accepted in principle. If your dog - usually when out for a walk - has picked up something that you want him to spit out, then, in addition to the command "Give," an exchange of "prey" is a good idea. In doing so, you offer the dog a treat, for example, which he only gets as soon as he gives away his prey.

Staying alone

You should train your dog in small steps to stay alone. If you go out without your dog, avoid saying goodbye. Your leaving and coming back should be a normal action for the dog. With a puppy, you first test being alone by leaving the apartment/house and closing the door, but after a short time opening it again and returning. If this works well, you can, for example, take out the rubbish and come back after a few minutes. The time to return is then regularly increased, and soon it should be possible to go shopping for half an hour and leave the puppy alone during this time. We did the same with our dog Merlin, and, in the end, he stayed alone for up to 6 hours without any problems – during which our five cats always kept him company. If your dog is well-behaved and, above all, quiet (without barking and without wreaking havoc) in your absence, you can test for a longer period of time in exceptional cases. The individual approach to being alone also depends to some extent on the breed and character of the dog.

If you have fixed times to go out for a walk and your dog gets loose in the process, that's great. However, you should bear in mind that sometimes he doesn't have to do his business at the same time as usual. Especially if you have health problems, such as stomach problems or diarrhoea, you should not lock your dog up for too many hours alone at home.

Because we know that our Merlin has a sensitive stomach, and in order to avoid unpleasant events in the house, 5 hours was usually the maximum for his being alone. At this point, I would like to tell you briefly about what happened when we once left Merlin alone for almost 7 hours. During this time he would have had to go outdoors urgently in order to do his big business there. But since we were not at home, this happened in the house. Unfortunately, the business was additionally very thin, because Merlin had apparently tried for a very long time to hold back the bowel movement.

If once such a fragrant event happens, you should not yell at your dog or even punish him. He can't help it if there is no one there for him to show that he urgently needs to get out. It is best to remove the fragrant happening without comment and then go for a walk with your dog or you can let him go out into the garden immediately after you come home, if available.

Note: If you are away from home for several hours, always provide your dog with a full bowl of fresh water. Because of our six pets in the house, we usually have even three bowls of water.

Rewards for a successful education

When training your dog, you should always work with positive and negative reinforcement. This means that desired behavior is rewarded immediately and to unwanted behavior you immediately react with rejection or ignorance (this depends on the individual situation).

Education also often goes through the stomach, and this brings me to the topic of treats. Treats that are used in moderation and in direct relation to praise for positive behavior result in very good and positive conditioning. Please also do not forget to include the reward in the general nutrition plan. My experience on overweight dogs: As Merlin one day weighed 59 kg, the vet advised us that he should lose weight to protect his joints and to positively effect his general health. We have easily managed the weight loss through longer walks and especially by reducing treats and his two food rations (1 in the morning, 1 in the evening). We weigh the food rations with a kitchen scale so that he always eats the same amount and now Merlin consistently weighs 10 kg less.

But feeding treats constantly is not the only effective reward. Dogs are even more happy about positive reactions such as your spoken praise and extensive petting. If you already know your dog well, then you know which gifts he particularly likes and you can use these specifically to reward a desired behavior. Merlin, for example, loves it  and is totally relaxed when you massage his neck and back. We ourselves can also let our thoughts wander during this massage, with the focus on Merlin's well-being - so dog and man both benefit from this "reward."

If your dog has done something well and satisfactorily, show him clearly by your behavior and voice, regardless of giving a treat. If he has done something wrong, then your voice will just as well prove to be a "punishment." You can also turn away from your dog and leave him alone if he gets too rough, for example when playing. This happened with Merlin from time to time, he sometimes rocked himself up and became rowdy. By turning away from him, he learned that his wild behavior is taking away his attention and that it only brings him our ignorance. So he quickly calmed down again.

Fun and variety

Parallel to the reward, fun and variety must not be neglected - both are an important factor for your educational success. Monotonous methods do not lead to boredom and listlessness only in humans. You will have much more success in training your dog if you always try something new and offer your dog new stimuli. In any case, you should be aware that some dog breeds demand more from their owner than others in terms of variety. For example, if you have an active Border Collie or any other breed of herding dog, you should have a lot to keep him busy. Such breeds have been bred to take over the work of herding independently, to be with a herd all day and to supervise it carefully. Please also keep in mind that your dog will develop further. What a puppy or young dog used to enjoy in the past can bore an older and more experienced animal.

Communication

One of the most important criteria of successful dog training is functioning communication. The dog must listen to you and understand what you tell him and what you want him to do. As pack animals, dogs are used to communicating with their conspecifics. And dogs have learned in living together with humans to interpret human signals in their own way. An extremely important point is the timing!

If you want to reduce or reinforce a behavior, you must react immediately to the behavior. If you miss this - admittedly - short moment, your dog will no longer be able to make the connection between his behavior and your reaction to it. You should also make an effort to always give clear signals. A dog reacts to learned commands, but also to gestures, your tone of voice and your general mood. If your command says one thing and your gesture says another, you will create contradictory signals for your dog. As a result, your dog will not know what to do. For example, if you say "No" and at the same time signal inattention or disinterest, you risk that your command will not be taken seriously.

Two absolute no-gos in dog training: humanization and violence

These two things really have no place in dog training. Even if dogs have been domesticated for a very long time, they react instinctively and immediately to a situation. They do not think morally or logically. A dog feels most comfortable if you accept his animal characteristics and treat him accordingly. For education, you should consider how you react to undesirable behavior. One thing is for sure: **to educate a dog, you never have to be rough!** You can show the dog by your behavior alone or by an energetic command that you do not agree with something. In case of repeated or continual misconduct, a dog expert should be contacted. He can give you tips and advice on how you and your dog can live together without conflict.

Information about puppy school, young dog course and companion dog course

In a dog school, you and your dog can learn under expert guidance to deal with each other peacefully, to communicate successfully and to act as conflict-free as possible in a social environment. In the dog school, your dog learns to obey different commands in the context of dog training. At the same time, you can learn to give these commands in a way that your dog can understand.

Through the support in a dog school, it becomes easier to train "difficult" dogs, and the right way to act with such dogs is practiced. In this way, even in "difficult" dog-holder constellations, the happy coexistence of dog and owner is made possible. The prerequisite is, of course, that you actively apply the exercises shown and what you have learned. In addition, a dog can make contact with other dogs during a training course in the dog school, which has a positive effect on his current and future social behavior. There are dog schools that train on dog training grounds and sometimes there is also the possibility to train together in the open air or in suitable premises.

Puppy school

Most dog schools offer so-called puppy schools for dogs up to about the 16th (maximum 18th) week of life. These are play and learning lessons with dogs of the same age, where not only the puppies but also their humans can learn a lot. For example, the puppy will become accustomed to the world, which is so exciting for him, during excursions together, he can practice dealing with his conspecifics and he learns the most important rules of obedience. In puppy school, the most important phase of the dog's life should be used to positively influence his individual development. An early and consequent education based on reward instead of punishment will make your puppy a self-confident and friendly dog later on. In addition, the intensive involvement with your puppy promotes a close and understanding bond, from which you will both benefit in the long term.

Young dog course

After puppyhood, a young dog considers himself incredibly mature and adult, which of course he is in no way. You can change from the puppy group to the young dog group from about the 16th week of life. At the young dog age, many people do not recognize their dog, and now it is important to carry out the education with increased consequences. Suddenly, everything that has been learned so far is usually completely erased: Sit - Lie down - Heel - Come: what does that mean? In a young dog course, these basic commands are repeated regularly and consolidated for the future.

During the young dog period, many dogs seem to unite two characters in themselves. One time he is extremely brave, another time, totally jumpy - for example, when a loud noise is heard or something unexpected happens nearby. In this phase, it is necessary that you lead the dog in a sovereign manner and also promote his acceptance of the proximity of other dogs and humans.

You and your dog will learn in the course to cope with the various environmental stimuli and to successfully master critical situations. If your dog is well socialized, then later encounters with conspecifics or incidents that the environment dictates are less dangerous. And you will not get into an unwanted stressful situation, because you and your dog are trained and you have learned to handle him calmly.

Companion dog course

The companion dog course can be started from when a dog is 15 months old and is completed with the companion dog exam. If you pass this exam, you will receive a companion dog pass. This course is a basic training, which is designed to be purpose-oriented and is limited to the most important criteria in the coexistence of dog and man. The companion dog course is not a performance competition, but it is the prerequisite for various advanced courses, for example, in dog sports and special performance courses.

The examination covers three parts:
- expertise lessons with examination for mistress and/or master
- urban education (behavior in road traffic)
- basic training in obedience (line handling, run free, sit, lie down, recall, etc.).

Problems

It doesn't have to, but problems can arise when your dog has been with you for only a short time - especially within the first days and weeks. Maybe your dog is not housebroken or he does not stay alone or he destroys various things. Maybe he is just scared and needs a little time to settle in and feel comfortable in his new home. It is also possible that he makes himself comfortable in your bed and moans all night long in front of the closed bedroom door after you have kicked him out. It may be that he sticks to you so intensively from the first day that you cannot even go to the toilet without him. Maybe after a week he gets the idea that he should be responsible for the pack and refuses you or strangers access to the apartment or house. Or he barks like mad while you are driving, pulls terribly on the leash, inhales anything edible or is always in the way in your home, so that you constantly stumble over him.

Just about all these problems can be solved with patience, common sense and your consistent actions. Your dog simply does not (yet) know the rules of the game when he moves in with you. So you have to explain them to him first, because he won't figure them out by himself. Before you run out of ideas and are faced with "unsolvable" problems, get advice from a dog expert, because this is the only way to avoid major disasters.

Common misconceptions

At this point, I would like to mention a few misconceptions regarding the interpretation of dog behavior which are still very common. Most experienced dog owners are quite adept at reading the dog's body language and interpreting dog behavior correctly. However, confusion can sometimes arise when it comes to certain signals and behavior.

1. Young dogs have puppy protection

Nowadays, you still often hear that puppies or young dogs enjoy a protection that prevents adult dogs from handling them roughly or biting them. But the reality is different, because older dogs are usually annoyed when puppies are constantly jumping around in front of them, jumping at them or nibbling at them or even nipping them with their sharp milk teeth. Since puppies have no instinct about protection, they must be taught to behave with respect when meeting an older dog. This starts with you as the owner, which means that you should not let your puppy loose on the other dog immediately. Rather, ask first whether they are allowed to play with each other, and only then let the dogs romp together. While playing, it can happen that the older dog rebukes the younger one a little bit and the little one squeaks with fright. But as long as the older dog's actions are appropriate to the situation, your puppy will digest the rebuke well and learn the consequences of his overly impetuous behavior.

2. Tail wagging always signals joy

This interpretation is wrong. When dogs wag their tails, it primarily means arousal. This does not only mean joy, but also aggression or excitement. For example, a tail that is held up and wagged stiffly can indicate dominance or even aggression. Which mood the dog really is in, you can see if you additionally observe other parts of the body. For example, if the dog puts his ears up, raises his fur or ducks while wagging his tail, there is not necessarily joy behind it. If you recognize the signals and interpret them correctly, you can avoid an unwanted scuffle or even a bite.

3. When coming home, a dog barks and jumps only because he is happy

Here, the exact opposite is the case. Of course, barking is a form of communication. However, if your quadruped does it when you come home, it often means one thing: he demands your full attention. If your dog jumps at you, this should be seen as a sign of disrespect. By the way, the same applies to jumping and running around while romping. In many cases, this is not due to carelessness or excitement, but rather, your dog deliberately testing his limits. From the beginning of your training, you should stop your dog's jumping. It is best to turn around and walk away. You can also pull up your knee before the dog jumps towards you and so interrupt the jump. Concerning barking: You can accept short barking, but if you hear continual barking or other unwanted actions, send your dog immediately to his assigned resting place.

4. If frightened dogs are over-cared-for, it increases their fear

This statement depends on the behavior of the person and his voice. If your voice pitch is different than normal, the dog will interpret this as if you were also afraid. This makes your dog feel confirmed in his behavior, which can lead to a permanent fear behavior. If your dog is afraid, you can go to him and pet him or cuddle with him - but try to be as you always are in your voice and behavior. This shows your dog that everything is fine and that he doesn't have to be afraid anymore.

5. What the dog has learned once, he will never forget

This statement is neither universally true, nor can it be denied for every dog. Some dogs are very obedient and want to please their mistress or master. That is why they are always very keen to implement what they have learned correctly. But there are also very headstrong dogs who test their limits again and again. In such cases, there is only one thing that helps: you have to repeat what you have learned continually and remind your dog of the established rules and guidelines. Often the "forgetting" of rules has to do with the phase of life of the dog, and so pubescent dogs in particular are sometimes very "hard of hearing" and difficult.

Tips for calming down during a thunderstorm and on New Year's Eve

Since there are several thunderstorms each year and at the end of each year there are exuberant New Year's Eve celebrations with banging firecrackers and rockets, I would like to show you here a few variations on how your dog can best survive these situations.

1. Call your dog to you

If you are outdoors, a thunderstorm is approaching and your dog is running free, you should call your dog to you and keep him on a leash. A bright lightning bolt and loud thunder can cause him to become frightened and panic. In such a situation, the dog often does not hear your calls anymore. The same is true on the days just before New Year's Eve and on New Year's Day, when rockets and firecrackers can frighten your dog. You can never know when and where a firecracker or rocket will be ignited and how panicky your dog will be in reaction to it. If we wanted to celebrate the turn of the year out, then we brought our Merlin to the parents-in-law, so he always had contact with people who were familiar to him. Before the beginning of the big fireworks, he was let outside at the latest at 10 o'clock for the last time into the well-fenced garden. I mention the fence because many a dog has jumped over the garden fence in fright and fled from the noise. This means that if your dog is allowed into the garden, the fence should be tight and high enough so that he cannot get over it. If you want to be on the safe side, you should also put your dog on a leash in the garden on New Year's Eve as a precaution.

2. Take away your dog's fear

As already mentioned before in the text about the five common misconceptions, the fear of a dog is not increased if you deal with it correctly. Speak in a calm voice and make calming gestures; you radiate calmness and normality, and that is the most important thing: be as normal as possible!

3. Give your dog security and safety

During a thunderstorm, dogs instinctively look for a safe place - usually a place to hide and shelter. This can be under a bed, chair, table or sofa. Some dogs also cower in a corner or seek shelter under hanging furniture or in an open cupboard. Alternatively, you can build a den for your dog, for example, by putting a blanket over the dog basket, under which your dog can then hide. You can also build a den of cushions on the sofa. The main thing is that your dog gets a chance to retreat.

4.   Protect your dog from lightning and thunder

To do this, close the curtains and lower the blinds or shutters. This will not only keep out the lightning (or New Year's Eve rockets) but will also reduce the sound of thunder (or New Year's Eve firecrackers). Another preventive measure would be to amplify distracting noises, such as those from the television or a radio.

5.   Use tranquilizers in an emergency

For the treatment of anxiety, there are helpful herbal and homeopathic remedies. You should consider these above all if your gentle voice, loving touches and the other measures mentioned do not give your dog peace of mind. However, tranquilizers should be the last resort to deal with a state of anxiety or panic. Be sure to speak to your vet to find out if and which tranquilizers can be used. Never try out any household remedies on your own that may work on humans but which could seriously endanger your dog!

Excursus to the topic: What a dog doesn't need and doesn`t like

A dog is and remains a dog - in other words, an animal. For this reason, dogs do not need a hairdresser or perfumed coat care. They don't need a dog hotel with a whirlpool and specially made dog furniture. They don't need rhinestone coats, shoes or caps. And since dogs usually have four legs, they don't need someone to carry them around in a bag. Besides, it is difficult to do the small or big business in this bag, just in case that it has to be done.

Dogs should be given the opportunity to get dirty, dig holes or maybe run around in the rain every now and then. If the dog is denied all this, it is against his nature. A dog doesn't need to be bathed every day to get a fluffy coat or be groomed for hours to look good when out walking. Even if the dog is man's best friend, he doesn't have to be with us everywhere. Sometimes you don't do the dog any favors by taking him everywhere with you. Visits to big celebrations, fairs or the Christmas market are better enjoyed alone. Dogs are extremely sensitive and perceive an incredible amount of their surroundings. In a crowd of people there are too many impressions that they cannot process. On top of that, they might be constantly jostled in the crowd or in the worst case even kicked - none of us want that, do we?

As far as communicating with a dog is concerned, you don't have to constantly chat with him. Sure, some people like to talk, often without a point and comma. Dogs are forced into the role of listeners, after all they don't talk back. Dogs turn their heads when we babble and generally give us the feeling that they understand us. Actually the dog is either stressed or insecure in such a situation. Dogs do not understand human babble and they do not know what to do with it. Does what I say apply to them? Should they carry out any command? If you don't want to confuse your dog and prevent him from not listening to you at all, you should avoid long chats. When communicating with your dog, it is better to use few, clear words and gestures. Because the dog understands these much better than our chatter.

If you communicate with your dog, this should also take place without too much eye contact. A dog can perceive an intensive eye contact as a threat. Among dogs you stare into each other's eyes especially when it almost comes to an argument. In this case, staring is a test of strength before a fight may occur in which the dog must defend itself. If you know this as a human being, you understand better why dogs avoid our gaze. If they turn their head to the side, they calm down and they tell us: Hey, I don't want any trouble. So we'd better save that deep look in the eye for other people.

Another human behavior that some dogs don't like is clinging hugs. If you know a little bit about the body language of dogs, you can see if a dog is happy with the hug. If the dog sits rigidly, has its head turned away, pants or even pulls its lips up, this is a sign of stress. This kind of physicality is too much of a good thing for the dog and is not pleasant, he tends to feel extremely oppressed.

You should also know that stroking the head or perhaps even constant patting is not perceived as pleasant by every dog. In such a case, stroking is neither an expression of love for the dog nor a reward for desirable behavior or for calming him down. Some dogs find patting on the head as unpleasant as we would. Let's be honest: Do we ourselves find being patted on our head great?

If you stroke a dog's head or pat him there although he does not like it, this can have consequences. If the dog does not (want to) endure it, he will try to escape the situation. If he is not able to do so, you will usually get corresponding (warning) signs such as a short lifting of the lips, visible teeth snarling or an audible growl. If these signs are ignored and the dog does not know how to help himself in any other way, he will sooner or later resist - be it by snapping, or, in the worst case, by a bite.

Foreign "strokers" in particular should know that a hand coming from above is a dominant gesture. This is similar to a dog that places himself above another dog and thereby wants to appease or even subdue him. If, in addition, one bends over the dog, this is a threatening situation for the dog. As when stroking, many dogs then turn their head away and try to evade the person. Here also, it is important to pay close attention to the behavior of the dog and not to ignore his evasive maneuvers, so that an escalation can be prevented. Dogs are also sensitive when you argue with someone. They sometimes get scared and retreat during the fight. Some dogs start to tremble because they are overwhelmed by the situation. They do not understand when, for example, mistress and master yell at each other. But it can also happen that the dog behaves aggressively towards your quarreling partner, because he wants to protect you. In any case, dogs have a very fine feeling for moods and if there is thick air, it can be really bad for them.

Excursus to the topic: Social compatibility

It has already happened to me and you will also hear from other dog owners that they were spoken to stupidly when they wanted to walk their dog without direct contact to another dog. In such a situation people sometimes say things like, "Your dog is probably badly socialized."

Such statements are intended to suggest that one has failed in the education of one's own dog, if he does not behave in a friendly way towards another dog in every situation. By the other dog owner's comment, one is subject to pressure to educate one's own dog to behave in a friendly manner and be ready to play with any other dog. On top of that, it can be suggested that your dog should perhaps also ignore the aggressive behavior of other dogs. This attitude is often supported with the argument that dogs are pack animals. Even if there are dogs that are just like that, this interpretation of "social compatibility" is a misconception that many dogs can never fulfill. Dogs know nothing of the human definition of social compatibility. And let's be honest, what kind of person likes every other person? So here, humans have a higher moral standard for a dog than we have for ourselves, and, in addition we apply a human moral standard to a dog which humans often don't abide by themselves.

This is unfair and ignores the fact that the dog is a domesticated predator. So what should one expect from a predator when he meets a foreign predator? If you think that your own dog will always remain friendly without any guidance from his owner and never get into conflict, then you have unrealistic expectations of your dog.

Social compatibility has nothing to do with the behavior when a dog leaves his owner when meeting another dog, ignores every call and harasses the strange dog, for example, with game requests. Social compatibility also has nothing to do with a dog lying flat on the ground in a lurking position, staring at oncoming dogs and then suddenly rushing at them. Anyone who lets his dog get away with such behavior is anything but "socially acceptable," even as his owner. The social compatibility of one's dog begins first with the owner, with the attitude that nobody should be molested. Strictly speaking, social compatibility is the neutrality of the dog towards his environment. This means that the dog does not react in an excessively friendly or aggressive manner towards strangers or other dogs - simply neutral, as if they were not even there. In this way, the dog is neither a nuisance nor a risk for other people and their dogs.

Just like a human being, a dog can reject physical contact with other dogs. And this does not have to be because the dog had bad experiences with other dogs. It is also not because you as the owner have failed in education. You cannot change your dog's attitude towards other dogs with education. And you cannot teach him to like every dog he meets or change his character. Yet you can teach him to take care of you and simply ignore other dogs. But this ignoring only works as long as no direct contact is forced by the other dog. Dog owners who speak of poor socialization should think about how they would react if a person who is unpleasant to them forced contact with them. Are they then also poorly socialized?

Excursus to the topic: My dog is attacked by another dog

Here, I would like to go into a topic that will occupy every dog owner at some point during walks. If you think about it in advance, you are better prepared and can react in a "cooler" way. It is about the fact that when you go for a walk, you sometimes meet aggressive strange dogs. This is less of a problem if both dogs are on a leash, because then you can either completely avoid the other dog or at least avoid an attack, if, after an initially calm sniffing, you see that the other dog might grab your dog and bite him.

As a rule, no dog attacks another dog because it enjoys proving its superiority. Aggression is not a problem of "alpha dogs", but rather a problem of dogs that feel insecure and uncomfortable. One of the most common causes of aggressive behavior towards strangers is that your dog senses that you are insecure and therefore believes he needs to defend and protect you. If you get nervous when another walker approaches you with your dog and you fear that your dog will start barking aggressively as soon as you approach him, your dog will sense this and eventually show this behavior.

Your well-intentioned attempts to calm your dog down through increased coaxing or stroking will confirm your dog's behavior. It is best to draw your dog's attention to you, for example with a treat. But you should only give him this after you have passed the other dog.

I would like to point out that in towns as well as on mountains, it is usually compulsory to keep dogs on a leash and in areas outside the town (forests, nature reserves) there are corresponding signs indicating that a leash may be compulsory. Nevertheless, some dog owners do not comply with this and some unfortunately do not comply at all or comply late with the request to keep their dog on a leash. So you may come across dog owners who let their dog run free and make no effort to leash it, even though you are walking your own dog on a leash. In such cases, the free-roaming dog may suddenly attack your dog.

If your dog is attacked by another dog and the other owner is not in sight or reacts too late, then try to fend off the other dog before he reaches you and your dog. This defense can be done by calling out loudly in a threatening voice or by throwing, for example, a bunch of keys or another rattling object. It would be  practical if you always have such a noisy object with you when you go for a walk. You can also use the same object very well with your own dog, if, for example, he wants to pick something up and you stop him by throwing the loud object (in addition to saying "Fie" or "No"). Of course, you should not throw the loud object at your own or at the other dog, but just in front of him on the ground. If the dog is attacking, you can also make yourself taller by standing upright and stretching your arms upwards to make yourself look even more imposing to the attacker.

If all this does not help, you should - if the environment allows it - give your dog the opportunity to escape and let him off the leash or run away completely with the leash. What you should never do is to run away with your dog - as mentioned before, this escape behavior only reinforces the hunting instinct of the other dog. If you have a small dog, you should also never lift him up and hold him in your arms - you risk being bitten yourself, and you may let your dog fall to the ground in fright.

If you were able to let your dog off the leash, you should keep a cool head and watch what happens next. It will become clear whether it is a harmless show fight or a serious fight with the intention of hurting or even killing your dog. An indication of the seriousness of the situation is the posture of the attacker. If he stiffens up, the hairs on his neck rise and he fixes your dog with his gaze, he shows very aggressive potential. In this situation, a wagging tail underlines the aggressiveness and the dog will not make a sound but will attack and fight fiercely. At this moment, your dog will hardly bark or growl, but will invest all his energy in the upcoming fight, just like the attacker.

In a show fight, it all looks very different. The dogs are usually quite loud, they bark and growl audibly. In this case, you have the best chance to separate the dogs from each other quickly. A variant would be that both dog owners withdraw from their dog and go away visibly from their dogs. If the "mental" support of the master or mistress is missing, the attacker may get rather cold feet and retreat.

If you can't let your dog off the leash and the other dog attacks yours, try to keep calm nevertheless. If the other dog owner is nearby, he might be on the spot before a fight or attack takes place. If the attack has already started, you can keep smaller dogs away in an emergency by defensive punches or kicks, but this will not help much with larger dogs. In addition, the attacking dog may become even more aggressive and attack not only your dog but you as well. The best thing to do is to call the owner of the other dog and ask him to help you, put his dog on the leash and take him away. This should normally be done by the other dog owner without any special request. If in the (very rare) extreme case the other dog has bitten your dog, you can try to lever the two apart. But for this you need two people, optimally the other dog owner and you, because you know your dogs best.

For levering, each dog must be taken by the hind legs and held firmly. Then both dogs have to be pushed into each other strongly, lifted briefly and then pulled back at the same time. This action requires that the other dog owner and you coordinate and think carefully and act simultaneously. If your dogs are biting each other, you must never simply pull them apart, as this can cause serious injuries. If the biting dog wears a collar and does not let go of your dog, you can try - but only in an absolute and extreme emergency - to cut off his air supply by narrowing his collar. You can also use your dog's leash on the other dog for this purpose. If a dog cannot breathe, he will normally cease the attack. What you should never do, however, is carry and use a stun gun, a knife or a pepper spray - all these things should never be used against a dog! They also carry the danger of hurting you. By the way, in 9 years with my dog Merlin, such an extreme situation has never happened to me personally, and, as a rule, I was always well able to avoid an impending escalation with bad consequences by local evasion or by defense with a loud voice.

Excursus to the topic: "Mounting" or "Shagging"

If a dog "mounts" or "shags" another dog, this can have several reasons. In dogs and bitches this happens mainly for the very natural reason of reproduction. However, if the mounting happens with conspecifics of the same sex, there are other aspects to consider. For example, the occurrence can be interpreted as a skipping action or stress reduction. If a dog is excited, overwhelmed by a situation or in conflict between different behaviors (such as: going or running away), it will from time to time spontaneously choose an apparently inappropriate behavior. This skipping action can then be, for example "mounting" or "shagging". "Mounting" or "shagging" can also be a kind of social interaction, for example when the game is abandoned, aggressive behavior, showing off or defending resources. Contrary to frequent assumptions, mounting is not a dominant behavior. Nevertheless, the situation and the behavior of both dogs should be closely observed and the mounting should be stopped as soon as possible.

Should the dog shag your leg or on the leg of someone else, do not simply push the dog away. Take him off his leg and direct his attention to something else. This way you can, for example, interrupt and stop the mounting by setting a task.

Crash course on education (especially for puppies and young dogs)

Learning the name: To teach the name, you should always combine saying the name with something positive, such as giving a treat immediately. Say the name and when your dog responds, give him a treat. Repeat this exercise several times a day and soon your dog will know his name and react when you call him.

Practise the command "Off": Off is a stop signal and it is important that your dog knows it reliably, for example, when the dog has something in its mouth that it should let go of. You can practise it very well during play. When the dog has a toy in its mouth and is supposed to give it up, you say "Off". When he opens his mouth, you take the toy and give him a treat. Then give him his toy right back so that he sees that he will get it back. You can also practise the command "Out" when he has something forbidden in his mouth and has to spit it out. In this case, of course, he only gets a treat as a reward.

Learning the command "blanket" (send to a place): This is very important, for example, when you want to eat in peace or when you have visitors and the dog has to be quiet. For this exercise you need a fixed place to lie down, for example a blanket or a dog bed, onto which you lure your dog by throwing a treat onto the place. You automatically make an arm movement in the direction of the place, which also gives your dog a non-verbal hint to the blanket. Repeat this several times and your dog will learn that this place is great because there is always a treat there.

Practise the command "Here": The best time to practise this is when your dog is a few metres away from you and is walking towards you on his own. At this moment, call "Here" immediately and when your dog is with you, give him a treat. Do not hold the dog, but let him decide for himself whether he wants to stay with you or not. Practice this command several times a day, because it is the most important command your dog has to learn. If your dog is allowed to run without a leash, he must listen to the command "Here" without hesitation if he is in danger, for example from cars, cyclists or other dogs. But you must also make sure that you can reliably call your dog to you when you see passers-by.

Practise the command "Sit": You might want to combine this command with the command "Here", because your dog might sit down in front of you after coming here. At that moment, while the dog is still sitting down, say "Sit" immediately and give the dog a treat. Otherwise, you can say the command

"Sit" whenever your dog sits down by itself, no matter where it is. However, you must give the dog a treat as a reward for sitting down.

Avoid unconscious confirmation: An unconscious confirmation would be if your dog jumps up at you or at someone else and then gets attention by looking at you, talking to you and petting you. In order for your dog not to achieve this goal and stop jumping, it must be consistently ignored. If this doesn't work, then make him "sit" as a substitute or send him to his blanket. You can also leash your dog before someone comes to visit. When the person is there, stand on the leash in such a way that your dog cannot run up to your visitor or jump on him. You can also use this restriction with the leash when you are talking to someone on a walk and your dog feels that he absolutely has to draw attention to himself. If you stand on the leash and your dog is consistently ignored by the other person and you, he will calm down after a short time.

No contact with leashed dogs: Dogs should not have contact with each other when both are on a leash. If, during a walk, your dog sees another dog and therefore starts to pull on the leash and you allow him to pull, your dog will learn that he is successful in pulling. You can prevent pulling by standing still, maybe letting your dog sit or standing on the leash. Then distract your dog from the other dog with a very tempting treat until the other dog has passed. You can do this in the same way if your dog pulls towards other people (without a dog), cyclists or joggers or even jumps in their direction. It is best to stop so that you are between the dog and the other person and distract the dog with a treat until the person is gone.

Avoiding contact with another leashed dog is not necessarily just avoiding a possible scuffle. It may be that the other dog is sick, old or not compatible with strange dogs. On a leash, dogs cannot communicate properly with each other, they cannot use their body language and they cannot avoid each other. This means more potential for conflict than an off-leash meeting. If you have your own dog on a leash but a strange dog runs free and towards your dog, ask the owner to put his dog on a leash and try to keep the other dog away from yours. You can block him, for example, by taking a step towards him and giving him the command "Go away". If this does not work, the chapter "Excursus on the topic: My dog is being attacked by another dog" describes instructions for emergencies.

Basically, when it comes to training, consistency is the most important thing and you should never rely on the motto "learned is learned" with puppies and young dogs. Learning and practising is a constant process that can take several years, depending on the dog.

CHAPTER 7: Health

Nutrition

There are many different views and opinions on this topic. As a dog owner, you naturally ask yourself: how do I feed my dog correctly? In any case, you should not feed your dog a single complete food for the rest of his life. By changing your dog's diet regularly - also depending on his age or a possibly necessary diet - you make sure that he gets a balanced, and, above all, varied diet. You also prevent the danger that your dog becomes too accustomed to one special type of food and then wants to eat only this one type. You can also provide variety by supplementing his food with, for example, rice, potatoes, vegetables (e.g., beets, cooked corn) or low-fat curd cheese. If your dog also eats fruit, you can cut an apple into small pieces and mix it into the food. WARNING: Never give your dog spicy food!

It is also possible to eat only home-prepared food. Many dog owners use the feeding variant "Barf." "BARF" stands for Biologically Appropriate Raw Food. Here, the dog is fed raw meat and vegetables. This method of preparation is intended to come closer to the nature of the animals as carnivores than the usual food mixtures. Although this type of food is free of industrial additives, the preparation requires nutritional knowledge and more time to prepare a truly balanced diet of proteins, fats, carbohydrates, minerals, trace elements and vitamins. If you decide to prepare the food for your four-legged friend yourself, you should definitely read the relevant literature beforehand and then consult a vet. Often, dog owners always use the same ingredients, and this can lead to one-sidedness, which can result in a lack or excess of essential nutrients. It is advisable to draw up a scientific ration plan.

Please note: The "Barf" menus available in pet shops can be a risk factor in the transmission of bacteria that are resistant to antibiotics and can thus cause dangerous diseases. This was the conclusion reached by researchers from the University of Zurich in a study published in October 2019 (see website https://www.media.uzh.ch/en/Press-Releases/2019/Barfen.html). With regard to the provision of water, please ensure that your dog gets fresh water at least once a day. In addition, the water bowl should be cleaned regularly. We always have two to three water bowls in use for our dogs and cats.

Merlin has an additional bowl of water outside on the terrace, which is also filled with fresh water every day and cleaned regularly. During the cold season, especially in winter when it is very cold, we also change the water every time we let Merlin out into the garden. We have found that Merlin's stomach does not tolerate ice-cold water very well and therefore we always take a pot of fresh, lukewarm tap water with us when we go out.

Vegetarian food? Yes, but not permanently.

As long as an adult dog, for example, does not need a special food due to a certain illness and eats "everything," so to speak, he can be given a varied diet of milk and egg products, vegetables, rice and pasta. In principle, it is possible to feed a dog a vegetarian diet. However, in order to prevent malnutrition in the long term, the composition of the food must be balanced. This means that the energy and protein requirements, as well as the need for all minerals and vitamins, must be covered and the ingredients must be in a balanced ratio.

A veterinarian should always be consulted when choosing a suitable food for growing, sick or old dogs. He should be involved in deciding which food is optimal for your dog at that time of his life or special life situation. When choosing food, you should not ignore the behavior of your dog and his species: the dog is a carnivore - that means he likes to eat meat!

For this reason, meat should never be completely avoided in the diet, even if there is no reason why the dog should not be fed a vegetarian diet in between. We have fed Merlin mainly with dry food and have had very good experiences with it. We divide his daily feed ration: One ration is fed in the morning and one ration in the evening, both always at the same time. Now and then he also gets fresh (uncooked) beef, but not raw pork, because it can contain threadworms or viruses. In the worst case, this can end with a deadly infection.

Our experience with Merlin: We have fed him mostly dry food and had very good experiences with it. We divide his daily food ration: One ration is fed in the morning and one ration in the evening, both always at the same time. Now and then he gets fresh (uncooked) beef, but not raw pork because it can contain threadworms or viruses. In the worst case, this ends in a fatal infection.

Merlin occasionally gets a raw and uncooked beef bone to brush his teeth. Attention: Bones must always be fed raw, raw chicken bones are also ok, contrary to earlier opinions. However, please never feed cooked, grilled or otherwise heated bones, with these there is a high risk that they splinter! Bone splinters can pierce the intestinal walls, causing food particles to enter the abdominal cavity and cause inflammation. When feeding bones, be sure to watch the dog's bowel movements. Too much bone can cause constipation, too much cartilage can cause diarrhea in some cases.

Vaccinations

Of course you want your dog to be healthy. To ensure that this is guaranteed for years to come and to prevent your dog from contracting dangerous infectious diseases such as parvovirus, he should be vaccinated. Veterinarians disagree about the right time and the number of repetitions, and dog owners are therefore often confused.

Vaccinations for dogs last several years

It has now been scientifically proven that the vaccination effect lasts for several years and not just one year. The "WSAVA" (World Small Animal Veterinary Association) has published certain guidelines on the subject of vaccination, which show that many vaccinations last for a few years and sometimes even a dog's life. Constant revaccinations can put a strain on an animal's body and increase the risk of vaccine sarcomas (tumors), but not the protection provided by the vaccine.

Which vaccinations are useful?

Which vaccinations have to be carried out always depends on the age of the dog. A puppy, for example, has already received antibodies from his mother and these are active until about the 8th week of life. After that, according to the StIKo Vet (Standing Vaccination Commission Veterinary Medicine), the following vaccination scheme applies to dogs (status: 1st of February 2019):

- 8th week of life: parvovirosis + leptospirosis + distemper, possibly HCC (= hepatitis contagiosa canis)
- 12th week of life: parvovirosis + leptospirosis + distemper, possibly HCC and rabies
- 16th week of life: parvovirus + distemper, possibly HCC
- 15th month or after completion of the tooth change: rabies as a single vaccination (for some rabies vaccines a second immunization at 15 months of age is recommended in the instructions for use)
- If necessary: revaccinate for rabies every 3 years
- Titer determination every 2-3 years

Below you will find a short description of the four diseases mentioned above:

- **Parvovirus:** A viral disease that is highly contagious and still widespread in some regions. It is one of the most common infectious causes of death in dogs and can be transmitted via feces, vomit and saliva. This virus often affects puppies with inadequate protection - the reason for this is decreasing maternal antibody levels. In non-vaccinated dogs, the course of the disease can be severe or even fatal.
- **Leptospirosis:** A disease caused by bacteria (for example, in contaminated water or carrion) and widespread in dogs worldwide. It can be transmitted from dogs to humans. Infections with these bacteria can be fatal without vaccination.
- **Distemper:** A highly contagious infectious disease that primarily affects unvaccinated young dogs between 3 and 6 months of age. The virus is transmitted via contact with sick animals and their waste (urine, feces, nasal secretions, etc.). Distemper leads to various diseases, which mainly affect the respiratory tract, the gastrointestinal tract and the nervous system of the dog.

- **Hepatitis:** An infectious viral disease that affects the liver and can be spread via urine, feces and body secretions from infected dogs. In young and unvaccinated dogs, the inflammation of the liver can be fatal; in older dogs, chronic inflammation of the liver can develop.

Rabies vaccination

Even if many EU countries are considered to be rabies-free, rabies vaccination makes sense. In Germany, there is no general vaccination requirement, not even for rabies. However, if you plan to visit exhibitions or dog shows, or go abroad with your dog, a valid rabies vaccination is mandatory! The first rabies vaccination should be given at the earliest at the age of 3 months, better at the age of 6 months, or as a refresher after a completed change of teeth. If you want to visit dog shows or foreign countries, as mentioned before, the rabies vaccination must be updated every 3 years. Otherwise, an update of the rabies vaccination is not necessary. After these vaccinations, your dog is fully immunized. From this point on, you do not need to have your dog vaccinated for a while. According to the latest studies, the vaccinations last up to 9 years. By the way, vaccines for humans and animals are similar in structure and often come from the same manufacturer.

Titer determination

It makes sense to have a so-called "titer determination" carried out every 2 to 3 years. This involves taking blood from your dog to determine the amount of antibodies it contains. If the titer value is okay, then the dog does not need to be vaccinated again. If the titer value is too low (the duration of the vaccination protection depends on the vaccine), the vaccination must be updated.

Can a dog be "over vaccinated"?

Yes, this is possible, and too frequent revaccinations could damage the dog's immune system in individual cases. There can also be intolerances such as diarrhea or vomiting, up to and including autoimmune diseases, paralysis and meningitis. From time to time, so-called "vaccination sarcomas" form, i.e., tumors that appear at the vaccination site. Vaccinations can also sometimes cause allergies, immune deficiencies, arthrosis and diabetes. Unfortunately, research in this area is still very poor. In summary, it can be said that for many diseases, vaccination protection is available for years. Exceptions in the duration of protection are diseases caused by bacteria such as leptospirosis or kennel cough. However, these diseases can be treated well, and therefore a vaccination is not absolutely necessary. With these vaccinations, the risk of damaging the immune system is much higher than the benefit. The best thing is to clarify with your vet how often and against which diseases your dog should be vaccinated in the course of the next few years, because there are, as already mentioned, quite different opinions.

Deworming

As for deworming, it is recommended to do it twice a year for an adult dog. This is the recommendation of our veterinarian for a normal risk of infection and it can be found in the same way in reference books and internet sources. If worms are suspected, fecal samples can be given to the veterinarian, who will send them to a specialized laboratory for analysis. You can do a deworming quite easily by giving your dog tablets which are available from your vet. Dogs that are infested with fleas or eat a dead mouse during a walk or in the garden usually have worms, so you may need to deworm your dog more often.

Coat care

For a beautiful shiny coat that does not smell like a dog, not only a healthy diet but also regular brushing of the coat is important. If you have a puppy, it's best to get him used to brushing from an early age. Particularly if your dog has long hair like our Bernese Mountain Dog Merlin, you should brush the  coat several times a week. With regular grooming, you will not only prevent a shaggy or knotted coat, but also the accumulation of many new tufts of hair in your home in a very short time. At the same time, you can remove the dead hairs from the undercoat by brushing. This ensures that the coat is well aired, which your dog will thank you for in the hot season. We had Merlin's fur shorn short in the spring for a few years. But then we switched to brushing only, because this care of the coat and especially the undercoat is absolutely sufficient. There are many different types of brushes available in specialist shops, and we have acquired several variations over the years. The best thing is to get advice from a pet shop or to ask a dog groomer which type of brush is optimal for the care of your dog's coat.

Sometimes it may be necessary to wash your dog. Merlin's coat never stank and he rarely got very dirty, so we only washed him twice a year. The general rule for washing is: as rarely as possible, as often as necessary. When washing, please only use dog shampoo because its ingredients are specially adapted to the dog's skin. Dog skin is very different from human skin: it has a different pH value, is thinner and reacts more quickly to external stimuli. Please wash your dog at home in the bathtub or shower and spare him a visit to one of these newfangled "car washes" for dogs. Your dog will panic if he is locked in a tight box, doused with water and shampoo and then dried with hot air. In my opinion, this kind of dog washing is cruelty to animals and should be avoided at all costs!

Claw care

It may be that your dog's claws need to be trimmed from time to time. This is when they are not sufficiently worn down while walking. Now and again, your dog's two wolf claws may also need to be trimmed. The wolf claws are the first toes on the inside of the dog's hind legs which do not touch the ground when running. One can say that it is a "thumb," so to speak, which dogs have on their front legs in the same way. With our Merlin, we have the wolf claws trimmed twice a year by the vet. If you cut away too much when shortening the claw, you can catch the blood vessels in the claw and cause more or less strong bleeding. At the veterinarian, the shortening of the wolf claws is always done in no time and mostly without bloodshed.

Fleas and mites

If your dog is infested with fleas or other pests, you should take quick action against it for his sake and for yours. Fleas are clearly visible to the naked eye and can be controlled with products from the pet shop or supermarket. However, if your dog is suffering from mites, it is better to go to the vet and let him decide how to proceed.

Ticks

Ticks are particularly fond of forest edges and clearings, as well as deciduous and mixed forests. They can also be found in grass, bushes and roadsides. To preventively protect your dog from ticks, there are various products available besides the Lyme disease vaccine, such as spot-on preparations, collars, shampoos, oils, various extracts, contact antiparasitics or special chewable tablets. During the warmer months it may be that your dog brings home a tick after a walk. As long as the tick has not attached itself, you can remove it by brushing the fur, for example. If the tick has already bitten somewhere, it should be removed as quickly as possible, but always carefully. There are various possibilities for the removal of a tick (see list below). To ensure that you do not pull out any or at least only a few hairs from your dog, pull the coat a little apart at the affected area.

- Tick card: You can get this (including instructions for use) in pharmacies.
- Tweezers: If you do not have a tick card, you can use tweezers. Try to pull the whole tick out, together with the head.
- You can also remove the tick with your fingers. Carefully put the tick between your thumbnail and your index fingernail (as close as possible to the dog's skin) and pull the tick out carefully.

If parts of the tick remain in the skin, this is not serious. These parts are rejected by the body. Important: Do not put alcohol, oil or glue on the tick! The tick will "vomit" in its struggle not to suffocate, and this way, the pathogens get into the blood even faster. Watch your dog after you have removed the tick. Does he eat, drink and behave normally? Is there a distinct circular redness around the bite? If so, contact a vet as soon as possible!

Stomach

Whether it's diarrhea, vomiting or loss of appetite - something can quickly hit a dog's stomach. If your dog has diarrhea, then you should always take it seriously. The causes can be very diverse and therefore an exact diagnosis is difficult. In acute cases you should consult a veterinarian and consider what could have caused the diarrhea. Below you will find a list of possible causes for diarrhea:

- Too fast change of food to unfamiliar foods
- Eating too large a portion
- Spoiled food
- Unclean drinking water
- Food or water that is too cold (e.g. if the water bowl is left outside in winter)
- Intolerances or allergies
- Side effects of medication
- Poisoning from poisonous plants, poisonous bait or poisonous foods
- Stress or other psychological causes as a result of anxiety and nervousness
- viral infection
- Infection with giardia (small intestine parasites)
- Parasitic infestation by worms
- Chronic inflammation of the gastrointestinal tract
- Diseases of internal organs, cancer or tumors
- Hormonal diseases
- Ingested foreign bodies

When should the veterinarian be consulted?

If you can rule out a few causes in advance, this is valuable information for the veterinarian. He should be visited if the diarrhea lasts longer than 24 hours. Puppies and young dogs should be examined the same day because they dehydrate very quickly due to fluid loss. However, adult dogs that react with lassitude, loss of appetite, fever (> 40° Celsius), apathy or vomiting should also be examined by a veterinarian as soon as possible. The same applies to signs of poisoning with symptoms such as trembling, vomiting or bloody diarrhea. Basically, it is better to go to the vet once too often!

Important information on the topic of stomach torsion: This is a frequently occurring and life-threatening emergency! Mostly large breeds such as the Great Dane, the Boxer or the German Shepherd are affected by a twisted stomach. Gastric torsion often occurs after eating, because the filled stomach tends to turn more and this happens especially when the dog plays wildly or runs a lot after eating. If the stomach is twisted, the dog is restless and tries to vomit in vain. His stomach bloats up and is hard and painful. The rotation of the stomach also causes the blood vessels and nerves of the stomach to be squeezed and the stomach is no longer supplied with blood. The dog becomes increasingly weaker, starts panting, his circulation breaks down and the mucosa of his mouth is pale. A stomach twist in the dog must be operated on by a veterinarian as quickly as possible, otherwise it will be fatal.

Home remedies for diarrhea in dogs

If your dog has diarrhea and otherwise shows no other accompanying symptoms, then observe him for a few hours. During this time, you can use the home remedies mentioned below, which have proven to be an immediate treatment. The most important thing is that your dog gets enough fresh water and that he accepts it. Tip: With a few simple tests you can check if your dog still has enough fluid in his body or if he shows first signs of dehydration:
- Is his mouth mucosa still moist or is it already sticky dry and light pink?
- Skin fold test: When you lift a skin fold, does it reattach quickly (as would be normal) or is it slow to retract?
- Are the eyes clear and alert or do they appear dry and sunken?

What you can do

Boil drinking water: This will prevent your dog from picking up any more bacteria or contaminants from the water that could further stress the digestive tract.

Add activated charcoal to the food: Charcoal tablets or charcoal powder will help soothe your dog's intestines again. Activated charcoal has the ability to absorb toxins from the dog's intestines. For dosage, follow the manufacturer's instructions or call a veterinarian. Caution. Charcoal tablets are an important first aid measure in cases such as suspected poisoning, but you should still have the exact cause of your dog's diarrhea determined by a veterinarian as soon as possible.

Prepare a carrot soup: First, 500 grams of carrots are peeled and boiled in a liter of water for at least an hour. Then the soup is pureed and made up to one liter with water, a pinch of salt is added and provided to the dog in small portions throughout the day.

No treats and chews: Feeding treats and chews is not recommended during or shortly after acute diarrhea because they can overload the gastrointestinal tract and trigger diarrhea again. Similar to us humans, your dog should rather be fed with gentle food.

24-hour diet: Your dog does not get any food for at least 24 hours. This allows the gastrointestinal tract to recover and empty. However, make sure that your dog takes in enough liquid during this time, as this is lost through the food. If necessary, the dog must be encouraged to drink.

Gentle food: If your dog finds it difficult to accept the deprivation of food, then give him a special diet. This includes cooked rice, cooked lean chicken meat (without skin and bones!) and cottage cheese or curd. Attention: Some dogs do not tolerate lactose, so in this case dairy products should be avoided. You can buy ready-made gentle food flakes in stores.

Grated apple: In case of diarrhea, you can give your dog an unpeeled, grated apple, because the apple peel contains pectin. This substance binds water and helps to solidify the stool consistency and relieve diarrhea. The soluble plant fibers found in apples also stimulate the growth of "good" intestinal bacteria.

Feed fiber: If the consistency of the feces is very runny, fiber can help. Swelling plant fibers, such as psyllium, can absorb large amounts of water, providing immediate improvement. Psyllium is also suitable after acute diarrhea for intestinal rehabilitation and restoration of the intestinal flora.

Ears

It would be good if you practice regularly with the puppy from a very young age so that he can be examined inside his ears. It is important that his ears are not pulled or other pain is caused - the dog should not associate the ear-check with a negative experience. If you see that the ears are dirty, practice their gentle cleaning. I always use an unscented wet wipe (no cotton swabs!) and carefully clean the upper part of the ear with it. Please make sure that you really only clean the upper (visible) part of the ear so that the inner ear is not damaged, or your dog will find the cleaning unpleasant.

If your dog constantly scratches one ear and keeps shaking his head, this may be one of the causes: there are individual hairs in the auricle which can make the ear itch unpleasantly. If the hairs are located in the upper part of the auricle, they can be easily removed with a wet wipe. Otherwise, you have to wait until deeper lying itchy hairs migrate into the upper part of the auricle by themselves.

Scratching the ear and shaking the head can also mean that the ear is inflamed. This is indicated by the fact that the skin inside the ear is reddened. Normally the skin inside the ear is light pink; an inflamed ear is (dark) red on the inside. Have the redness checked by a vet, who can also prescribe a special solution to help the inflammation subside.

Teeth

Since dogs tend to have tartar build-up, it is important that you get your puppy used to having his teeth checked by you from a very early age. Tartar has the same consequences in dogs as in humans: in the beginning it is only an unsightly discoloration, then a firm, rough layer forms on the teeth, and

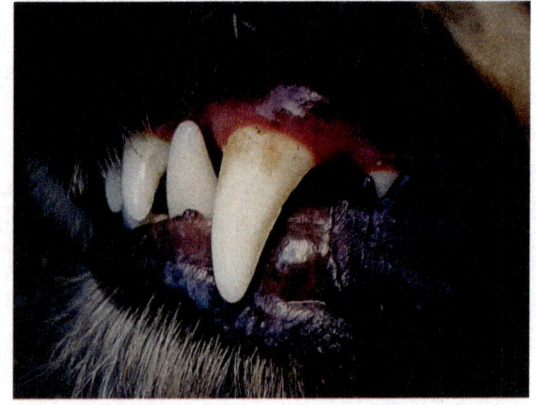

after that the teeth turn grayish yellow-brown. The plaque can spread over the whole tooth and subsequently inflame the gums underneath. Often many teeth, and, in the worst case, all teeth are affected. Further con-sequences of tartar can be: increased accumulation of bacteria, loss of teeth, chronic pain and bad smell. Tartar can be found in all dogs and dog sizes, as well as in all dog breeds and also in mixed breeds.

However, tartar is anatomically more common in smaller dogs with closely spaced teeth and a long narrow jaw. In small dogs, unlike large dogs, food debris accumulates more easily between the relatively narrow teeth and can cause bacteria and plaque. For example, Maltese, Yorkshire Terrier, and Shih Tzu have anatomically close standing teeth. Anatomically long narrow jaws are found in dachshunds and poodles. In general, the probability of tartar formation increases with increasing age in all dog breeds.

With the right diet, you can prevent plaque

Through wet food (canned food), the teeth are coated, so to speak, food residues remain in the spaces between the teeth, and greasy deposits form on the teeth. If tartar build-up is clearly visible due to wet food feeding, then switch to dry food. This can support the superficial cleaning of the teeth by the mechanical abrasion. In addition, you should completely remove sugary food from your dog's diet. Therefore, check the ingredients of purchased ready-to-eat food for sugar and also pay attention to the treats. Chewing sticks, buffalo hide bones, dried cattle scalp or bull whip also ensure clean teeth. Note: chewing items can be very high in calories and must be included in the daily feed ration!

Brush the dog's teeth regularly

To remove discoloration, you can give your dog an apple to bite on daily. If your dog has light plaque, you can playfully clean his teeth with appropriate toys. For example, use an old towel for a tugging game with your dog and let him bite into the towel. He will pull at it, and, at the same time, you can rub the towel over his teeth. Chewing ropes also support the cleaning of the teeth through their mechanical action, without your dog noticing. In pet shops you can also get teeth cleaning balls with special slats on which your dog can nibble and clean his teeth. To remove light tartar, you can also brush your dog's teeth with a special toothpaste and toothbrush. To do this, I would get the dog used to this type of teeth cleaning from an early age if possible. The removal of hard, mineral plaque or tartar should always be done by a veterinarian!

Paws

Dog paws are very sensitive, and serve, among other things, to regulate body temperature. They also absorb shocks and protect the joints from too much pressure. Get your dog used to you taking his paws in your hand from time to time and "examining" them. This helps when you visit the vet later, because the dog knows that nothing bad will happen when you examine his paws. This exercise is also the perfect preparation for cleaning and drying off any wet or dirty paws after a walk before getting into the car or at the front door. You don't have to bathe a dog with dirty paws every time - just put an old bath towel by the front door so that you have it ready to hand when you come home and can wipe the dirty paws immediately, before the floor gets a new pattern.

By the way, if you use caustic chemicals to clean the floor, this can have a negative effect on the dog's paws. Always use an animal-friendly and mild cleaning agent. In the middle of summer, you should remember that the asphalt on the pavement and on the street heats up greatly and the dog can burn his paws when walking. Therefore, either go for a walk early in the morning or after sunset when the asphalt has cooled down. You can test the temperature of the asphalt yourself in the evening by standing on it barefoot. If the ground is too hot for you, do not ask your dog to walk on it. Wait another 1-2 hours or take your dog for a walk in the countryside.

If your dog licks his paws excessively often, this could possibly mean a pH imbalance - one cause could be a lack of meat. If the paws are cracked, this could indicate a zinc deficiency, which can be remedied by adding fish oil directly to the food. If you put a bandage on your dog because of an injury, please remember to change it regularly. In winter, you should clean your dog's paws after every walk, because it's hard to avoid him walking on a salt-wet surface. Merlin got a gastro-enteritis from licking his salt-wet paws, which we had to have treated by the vet.

A note from our own experience: Our Merlin once indicated to us an injury by constantly licking a paw. Upon examining this paw, we discovered that one of the nails was splintered. This nail then had to be pulled at the vet and then grew back completely.

Anal glands

The anal glands are located next to the anal opening of the dog. They produce a strong-smelling odor secretion, which is secreted together with the feces. The smell of this secretion is present throughout the dog's territory and identifies the dog as the owner of the territory to a foreign dog. It can happen that the anal gland becomes clogged if the glandular secretion is too thick. When such a blockage occurs, the anal gland fills up, which causes an unpleasant feeling in the dog. Then, for example, he will slide along the floor while sitting or he will often lick his anus. The emptying of the anal gland is quickly done by a veterinarian and is an unproblematic procedure - but it leaves usually a quite strong smelling surgery.

Our experience with Merlin: as with various matters when he feels uncomfortable, Merlin starts "smacking" when the anal gland is clogged or he pretends to have hiccups. When Merlin behaves like this, we know that something is wrong. But every dog shows his discomfort in a different way. It is best to observe the dog closely, and, after some time, you know his behavior in certain situations (excitement, fear, pain) very well and you know how to interpret it correctly.

First aid tips

Of course, it is best to never get into a situation where your dog is in danger of his life - whether it is due to swallowing poisoned bait, a health problem such as a twisted stomach, a more serious injury while playing or a (traffic) accident. First of all, one thing is most important: you should keep calm, because panic does not help your dog, or you or any other person involved. Since there are many different situations that could require first aid and the description of each case would be too extensive, at this point, I would like to refer you to the German website www.erste-hilfe-beim-hund.de. You have to use Google Translator for this website, but you can also visit for example www.doghealth.com. On both websites you will find detailed information about life-threatening emergencies such as cardiac and respiratory arrest, heavy bleeding and suffocation attacks, as well as shock conditions.

In addition, acute emergencies such as bite wounds, poisoning by blue fertilizer or rat poison, intestinal obstruction or stomach torsion are also dealt with. Other acute emergencies may include sunstroke, heatstroke and broken bones. Of course, each emergency situation is described in detail about how to act best and what exactly you should do in each case. This includes the right measures to revive your dog. It is also highly recommended to attend a first aid course for dogs, which e.g. is offered by some veterinarians. There you will learn the first treatment of various injuries and how to deal with an emergency situation in general. In the following, In the following, I would like to address those emergencies that are most likely to arise: Poisoning, bite wounds, injuries to the paws and burns.

Tips for possible poisoning

The biggest danger is during a walk, because unfortunately there are always animal haters who deliberately prepare poisonous bait with apparent goodies to poison dogs. When you go for a walk, you should therefore keep your dog on a leash if possible - especially if you are walking in an area where there have been cases of poisoned bait being used. It is even better to choose another route for your walk. In any case, dog haters often choose "typical" walking routes in their own town, such as the main path in the park or the dirt road that runs along a stream. If your leashed dog stops during the walk to sniff at unfamiliar things, you can quickly look and intervene before he eats something. If it is already in his mouth, try to get it out again immediately - every second counts!

The best thing, of course, is to teach your dog to never pick up unknown things from the ground or accept things from strangers along the way. But this is a very difficult matter, and with our Merlin, we have not yet managed to do this, although we would have practiced it often enough in dog school. Therefore, we always keep a very close eye on what he is sniffing at and what he might want to eat.

An additional tip: If you are travelling in a foreign rural environment, make sure that your dog does not come into contact with a plant called giant hogweed. It is also called "Hercules" weed, grows on meadows and roadsides, has broad white flowers and grows 1.5 to 3 metres high. This plant is highly toxic and contact with it can cause redness, blistering, itching and other skin reactions. If you are out and about at ponds or other standing bodies of water, do not let your dog into the water, because it can be contaminated by blue-green algae, which are poisonous and can even be fatal for your dog if swallowed. Blue-green algae are also often found in lakes where many water birds are present.

General symptoms of poisoning

Usually a dog shows symptoms of poisoning such as vomiting, diarrhea or apathetic behavior. If you have noticed that your dog has eaten something unfamiliar in the garden or while walking, these symptoms are usually a strong indication of poisoning. External poisoning, for example, through contact with chemicals, is noticeable through skin rashes or blackened gums.

If the poison intake (e.g., eating slug pellets or rat poison) has just occurred, you can try to give your dog tablets made of medicinal charcoal to counteract the further progress of the poisoning. The charcoal is able to bind poison in the digestive tract and prevent it from being absorbed into the body. Nevertheless, in any case, take your dog to a vet immediately so that the vet can clarify the cause and possibly take life-saving measures!

If your dog has poisoned himself at home, for example by eating medication or by licking a puddle of cleaning fluid, it is best to take the cause of poisoning to the vet (for example, the packaging of the medication or the bottle of cleaning agent). This makes it easier for the vet to identify the toxin and take appropriate action quickly.

Tips for a bite wound

Externally, a bite wound from a scuffle can look harmless, but you should always examine your dog carefully. For this purpose, he should be kept on a leash and first of all be calmed. Panic does not help anyone in this situation. Maybe you should tie your dog up somewhere, so that you have both hands free for the examination. Please remember that your dog may be in a lot of pain and may snap at you during the examination, even if he is otherwise the dearest dog in the world. Therefore, it would be good for your self-protection if you put a muzzle or a muzzle sling on your dog at this time. Bite wounds can cause severe damage to the dogs affected by them. They range from two harmless-looking round holes, large gaping wounds, bruised and torn internal organs to a lung that collapses later. The very worst case would be an immediately fatal neck fracture.

Injuries that are barely visible at first glance, such as canines that have penetrated the body, sometimes leave only a punctiform injury to the skin on the surface, but can develop serious wound infections days or weeks later due to the introduction of wound germs. Contusions, in turn, can cause severe internal bleeding and hematomas (bruises). Tendon and muscle injuries may not be visible externally at first. After a scuffle, you should therefore always carefully examine and observe your dog for injuries. In the best case, you should have a vet take a look at the injury.

Tips for paw injuries

A dog puts strain on the paw bales with almost every movement when running and jumping, and, of course, when standing, the paw bales are always under strain. They are exposed to various injuries through thorns, sharp stones, shards, heat and much more. With a deep cut on the bale of the paw (for example from broken glass), the dog can lose a lot of blood. In addition, dirt in the wound can lead to protracted bacterial infections. No matter what happens, for a dog, problems with the paw bales are often very painful. As a first aid for your dog, you can try to remove any foreign bodies and then apply a paw bandage. Except in really minor cases, a vet should then look at the paw and decide on the next steps.

Tips for burn injuries

In contrast to human skin, the effects of burns are not so easy to detect - although they can have just as serious consequences. The most common burns are on the face, especially on the nose (keyword: sunburn) or on the paws, for example, when walking on hot asphalt in summer. At this time of year, it is therefore best to go for a walk early in the morning or late in the evening. If you suspect that your dog has burnt himself somewhere, cool the area with running water or put on a cooling cuff. If the area is under the coat, carefully remove the hair (with a dull pair of scissors or shave it off). This will make it easier for you to see any changes in the skin. For more severe burns, it is best to spray the wound site with a disinfectant spray, clean it carefully and then protect it with a sterile dressing. You should then have your dog examined by a vet immediately.

Further emergency cases

Another danger which exists when walking and which many people do not know about, is water poisoning. If your dog is a "water rat" and likes to play in the water, jumps into the water to fetch a stick thrown by you several times or swims for a long time, then you should make sure that he does not swallow too much water in the process.

Too much water can quickly become dangerous, because a dog should only drink a certain amount of liquid. If he drinks too much, he will cause his electrolyte balance to be out of balance. The dog stores water, salts and minerals in his body cells. If he swallows too much water in a short time, this  composition is no longer correct and certain bodily functions are disturbed. The kidneys can no longer filter out the water. The first symptoms can be dizziness, vomiting and loss of appetite. In the worst case, such water poisoning has fatal consequences.

There are also potential dangers lurking in your home in the form of various foods, cleaning products, plants or medicines. You should therefore always make sure that your dog is not able to absorb toxins, either consciously or unconsciously. For example, if you work with toxic household chemicals, you should always keep your dog away from this work area. In your own house and garden, you should also avoid using pesticides such as slug pellets and rat poison. Non-toxic alternatives to slug pellets are available in the shops today to control snails in the garden, and there are traps for rats.

The following (human) foods are poison for the dog and must never be fed to him: chocolate, grapes, raisins, onion, garlic, barley, chives, mushrooms, nuts, coffee, tea, cocoa, alcohol, sweetener, and salt.

To avoid flatulence and stomach ache, milk and dairy products, cabbage and broccoli should also be removed from the menu. Pork, beans and other legumes should all be fed cooked only. As mentioned elsewhere, bones should always be fed raw only, raw chicken bones are ok as well.

By the way, many plant species can also harm your dog. Many people are not even aware which poisonous plants "lurk" in the immediate vicinity of their dogs. For example, there are many poisonous house plants and garden plants that are so widespread that one cannot even imagine the great danger of poisoning a dog. If the dog nibbles or even eats a plant or root that is poisonous to him during some unobserved moment, the health risk and the danger of poisoning is very high. Even if the nibbling is only done out of boredom - especially with puppies that explore their environment with their teeth - the risk of poisoning from plants is particularly high. The consequences can be catastrophic, especially if the cause of the poisoning is not identified immediately.

You should keep your dog away from the following plants and not have them in the house or garden (the list is only an excerpt and is not complete): birch fig and all other ficus species, rubber tree, oleander, philodendron, all types of orchids, chrysanthemum, hydrangea, passion flower, azalea, amaryllis, cyclamen, window leaf, geranium, lilies, ivy, poinsettia and many others. Poisonous garden plants are also yew, wolfsbane, boxwood, angel trumpet, foxglove, laburnum, cherry laurel, larkspur, rhododendron, belladonna, juniper and cedar.

If you observe your dog eating or nibbling on a poisonous plant directly, take the plant away from him immediately or lure him away from the plant. If he has parts of the poisonous plant in his mouth and does not want to give them up, offer him something better (keyword: booty exchange). Offer him a treat or sausage - but of course he will only get it when he gives you the plant parts. If symptoms of poisoning occur or if the dog behaves strangely, take the dog to the vet and make sure to take the plant parts with you. Possibly the poisonous plant parts can help to identify the poison so the necessary countermeasures can be taken.

An event from our own experience: our Merlin has a bad stomach every now and then, and when we are at home, he shows us this - as already mentioned - by "smacking" and "swallowing," similar to a hiccup. When we are at home and see this, we let him out immediately into the garden where he eats grass and so he "puts his stomach back in order." Once we were out of the house longer than planned and he had a bad stomach, he could not go outside and then unfortunately started to eat the leaves of a monstera plant (window leaf) - poisonous for dogs.

As if that wasn't enough, he also bit off the threads from the curtain of the patio door and swallowed all the bitten off plant parts as well as the threads. The result was that when we came home, we found three huge piles of vomit in the apartment. On the one hand, this was very disgusting, but on the other hand, we were glad that he had got rid of the poisonous plant parts and the threads. We watched Merlin closely for the next few hours and the following day, and he showed no strange behavior.

So this episode went off without a visit to the vet. By the way, this was just as true when Merlin once in an unobserved moment in the garden ate several tit dumplings attached to a bush (including net), another time a dead pigeon and also once four packages of a chocolate snack (Kinderriegel) "stolen" from the living room table (including packaging). All these "meals" came - under constant observation of Merlin - thank God on the following days on "natural" way again to the appearance.

You see, a dog is an "omnivore," so to speak, and therefore you should always make sure that there is nothing lying around that he should not eat (whether packaged or unpackaged). If you have a big dog, remember that he can easily get to things that are on a higher table or on the sideboard in the kitchen. Merlin even once took Wiener sausages out of the sink, which we had put in there to defrost. Yes, dogs can be very resourceful when it comes to finding and "stealing" edible things.

Accidents while playing

One topic I would like to mention here is "stick throwing," which is very popular with many dog owners and their four-legged friends. In this game, you should make sure that the stick never has pointed ends, because your dog can hurt himself badly.

This is what happens when you throw the stick and it lands so that one sharp end gets stuck in the ground and the other sharp end sticks up. If your dog then runs to it and picks it up on the run, so to speak, it can happen that he pushes it down his throat. This can cause serious injuries. Even if your dog only chews on the stick, sharp splinters can come  loose, which, in turn, can injure the stomach and intestinal tract. The best thing to do is to replace the stick with a rubber or fabric object so that nothing can go wrong when he bites into it.

Diseases

In the course of his life, your dog will have "normal" health problems such as diarrhea, vomiting or coughing. It is possible that he will step on a piece of glass and may need stitches. It is also possible that your dog will be bitten by another dog at one time or another and may need stitches. And your dog may get an eye or ear infection. Apart from these "little things," your dog may also be affected by more serious illnesses as he gets older and may have problems with his heart, eyes or hips. Some breeds are also more susceptible to various types of cancer. Every serious illness causes not only grief, but also considerable (veterinary) costs - but your dog should be worth it and you should go through it together with him.

Fever

An elevated body temperature is a clear defense mechanism of the immune system in humans and animals. For example, if your dog has an inflammation in his body or an infectious disease, the body will defend itself against the pathogens with a fever. A fever is a sign that the immune system is functioning properly and that the pathogen is being fought. A dog's body temperature can vary depending on his size and age. In adult healthy dogs, temperatures between 37.5 and 39 degrees are normal; in puppies up to 39.5 degrees. If the temperature is higher than 40 degrees, this can become life-threatening. Please contact a vet immediately! Such a high temperature puts a strain on the organs and circulation. For this reason, a prolonged fever can lead to organ failure or circulatory collapse. Measuring fever is a way of checking your dog's vital signs.

You can tell whether your dog has a fever or not from various symptoms and accompanying signs. These can be:
- a dry nose (normally it is always slightly moist)
- excessive panting
- lack of appetite
- apathy
- hot ears (best felt on the inside of the ears)
- a hot body (palpable on the loins and on the inside of the thighs, in the armpits and also on the belly in the less hairy areas)

If you want to or have to take the temperature of your dog, it is advisable to practice this from an early age. The fever is measured in the anus. The measurement can be taken while the dog is standing or in a (stable) lateral position. Before taking his temperature, you should calm the dog down and perhaps put him on a leash or tie him up so that he does not run away. It is best to use a thermometer that you have bought just for your dog. Before taking his temperature, put some Vaseline or oil on the thermometer to make it more slippery, then lift the tail up and insert the thermometer about 2 centimeters into the anus. Hold the thermometer during the measurement. The duration for the measurement depends on the thermometer.

Check other vital signs

If you would like to check your dog's vital signs in an emergency, you can also take the following measures in addition to taking his temperature:

- To check the circulation, you can also measure the capillary filling time. Capillaries are the smallest blood vessels, and, with their help, you can see how the circulation is. If your dog is restless before the check, put a muzzle or a muzzle sling on him to be on the safe side. To check, push up one of his lips and press on a part of the oral mucosa or gums with your finger for a few seconds. When you take your finger off again, you immediately start counting the seconds while the area changes from white (due to the displaced blood) to pink/red (due to the blood flowing back). If there is nothing wrong with your dog's circulation, the pressed area should be pink/red again after about 3 seconds.

- If a lack of fluid or dehydration is suspected, place the dog on his side and pull the skin in the shoulder-neck area up to a crease. When you release the skin, the wrinkle should disappear immediately. If this does not happen, your dog must be taken to a vet or one called to visit immediately.

- Check the lymph nodes. Normally you cannot feel them. If you do feel them, you should have your dog examined by a vet.

- Check the mucous membrane of the mouth. It should be pink or red; any other color such as blue, gray or yellow indicates a circulation problem.

Special chapter on the subject of arthrosis

Osteoarthritis occurs predominantly in large and heavy breeds of dogs, they usually have a greater tendency to develop osteoarthritis than others. Our Merlin is one of them and that is why I would like to go into this topic in more detail. The positive news is that osteoarthritis can be prevented consciously, even if it cannot be prevented completely. But you should definitely do what you can.

Why preventing arthrosis is possible and important

Here I would like to give you a few concrete and practical tips that you can implement relatively easily in everyday life with your dog to prevent arthrosis.

1.   keep your dog's weight down and avoid overweight: Overweight dogs put unnecessary stress on joints and spine. No dog is helped by being

overweight. Excess weight always puts more stress on the joints and spine and should therefore be avoided at all costs - no matter how intense the begging dog look. In any case, you should still be able to see the hip and feel the ribs with your fingers with light pressure.

2.   have musculoskeletal problems and injuries treated by a vet immediately: Always consult a vet if there are problems with the musculoskeletal system! Possible conditions such as arthritis or an injury should not be left untreated for too long, setting the stage for arthritis. If your dog shows problems moving for more than 24 hours, then have your dog checked by a vet.

3.   build muscle and exercise consistently: Muscles support joints, this is the same in dogs and humans. But since you can't go to the gym with your dog, it is recommended to do some exercise together. Uniform movements are optimal for building muscles in dogs - preferably on a soft floor. If your dog is not a large or heavy breed, you can, for example, go jogging once a week for a few kilometres in the forest at a moderate pace. The ground is soft and you are both doing something for your muscles and joints without putting too much strain on them. It can also be great if your dog accompanies you while you ride your bike slowly - preferably also in the forest or near fields where your dog may be able to run off-leash. Please be careful not to set the pace too high or increase it too quickly. If it is warm outside and there is an opportunity near you, you can take your dog swimming. Swimming is great for dogs, it doesn't put unnecessary strain on the joints and yet the dog has to work hard, so the muscles are challenged and encouraged. This makes swimming particularly suitable for large or heavy breeds with whom you should not jog or cycle.

4.   avoid severe over-exertion: It is not that a dog should only run straight, not play and jump. But you should try to avoid most of the movements that put too much strain on his joints - this is especially true for growing puppies. Such overloads are, for example, sudden changes of direction, violent jumps up or down, or jerks such as sudden braking because the dog wants to catch the ball. Of course you can play ball and Frisbee, but only on surfaces and in a way that is not too violent. It is also better if your dog does not jump into or out of the car from an early age, always use a dog ramp for this.

5.   make sure your dog is lying down in a healthy position: It is also important that your dog lies down in the healthiest way possible. This is not an exaggeration, but a really important issue - after all, dogs sleep a lot of the day. And a dog that has pain in its joints cannot recover if it lies on a poorly produced dog bed that does not provide pressure relief for its joints and spine. We bought an expensive but first class orthopaedic dog bed for Merlin which helps him a lot.

6.   green-lipped mussel and devil's claw as a cure: green-lipped mussel and devil's claw are considered products that promote the maintenance of joints and synovial fluid. You can regularly add both to your dog's food as a cure. Even with a young dog, a cure helps to keep his musculoskeletal system and joints healthy. Unfortunately, our Merlin was diagnosed with arthrosis in his left hip when he was 10.5 years old, despite all our care (no mountain hikes, no extreme sports) and despite all preventive measures (ramp for the car and at home, food supplements). This arthrosis was due to his advanced age - for a Bernese mountain dog - and could be alleviated with painkillers.

Castration

At some point, there may come a time when you ask yourself whether or not you should have your dog neutered. There is no generally valid answer to this question, and opinions on this subject are usually quite divided. As already mentioned in chapter 3, neutering should basically only be done if there is a medical necessity for it. Neutering is the veterinary term for a procedure that removes the gonads from a dog (male dogs have their testicles removed; bitches have their ovaries, fallopian tubes, uterus and cervix removed). It is different from sterilization, where the veterinarian merely interrupts the spermatic ducts or fallopian tubes.

Castration is a final surgical procedure that cannot be reversed. It is performed under general anesthesia and can be accompanied by side effects. Before castration is performed, a thorough preliminary examination must take place. Only if the dog is healthy, can he be operated on. Since the hormones produced in the testicles and ovaries control the psychological and physical development of the dog, a dog should only be neutered after he or she has completed puberty. The sex hormones have an effect on the bone structure. Therefore, dogs neutered too early are more prone to joint problems and hip joint dysplasia.

You should only consider an early castration in exceptional cases, for example, if your dog has an abnormal sexuality or is aggressive, and after a detailed consultation with an expert. The length of puberty of a dog depends on his breed and various environmental factors and cannot be generalized. For example, large dog breeds need more time to reach adulthood. A bitch should not be neutered before her first heat. This way, you avoid undesirable coat changes and lifelong childlike behavior. One goal of neutering can also be to prevent unwanted reproduction. In addition, there are other reasons, which I will discuss below.

Worth knowing about castration of males

- In male dogs, castration can prevent not only testicular cancer but also some diseases of the prostate.
- A castrated male dog is usually calmer and has practically no sex drive.
- The encounter with a bitch in heat is much more relaxed.

Please remember that you cannot tame an aggressive male dog by castrating him. Although this is often claimed, it does not work in practice. If you have problems with your dog in this respect, then you should instead carry out suitable training with him.

Worth knowing about castration of females

- Castration can prevent uterine suppuration (pyometra) in bitches.
- The risk of the formation of tumors in the area of the milk ducts (mammary tumor prophylaxis) can be significantly reduced by castration. A mammary tumor is a tumor in the mammary crest, which is malignant in about 50 percent of cases. The pros and cons of prophylaxis by early castration should be considered thoroughly.
- An early castration (at the latest, before the second heat) helps to reduce the risk of breast cancer considerably.

In addition, a bitch can, of course, not come into heat again after castration. Typical behavioral changes, discharge and bleeding which accompany the heat will therefore not occur in the future.

Should you have decided to have a castration for your dog, please consider the following measures. Avoid long walks with your quadruped after the operation until the inner and outer wounds have completely healed. Always keep your dog on a short leash so that the wound does not stretch. Do not let your dog jump - not even from the couch or car seat. Check the wound daily to make sure it doesn't get infected. To prevent the male dog from licking the wound, it is best for him to wear a collar in the meantime, and the female dog to wear a special dog shirt.

We had Merlin neutered at the age of 1.5 years to prevent cancer. One day he suddenly had urine in his blood and the veterinary examination revealed that he had a cyst on his prostate. This cyst could be reduced by medication, but on the recommendation of the vet, we (with heavy hearts) had the castration done. I would have liked Merlin to be a proud daddy dog later on. With the castration, however, it was ensured that the cyst did not grow larger and possibly into a malignant cancer. And with the castration, at least the topic of cancer of the prostate or testicles was history once and for all.

CHAPTER 8: Our life with Merlin

In this chapter I would first like to tell you about the dog experiences I had as a child and teenager. Afterwards, you will learn how we live together with Merlin, the experiences we have shared with him, and his breed typical behavior. Bernese Mountain Dogs are generally known as comfortable and quiet companions, but can sometimes be quite stubborn. At such times, we have always said to ourselves that he has "character."

How I "got on the dog"

I gained my first dog experiences in 1984 at the age of 12 years, when my parents took a Cocker Spaniel bitch into the family. Because of her friendly nature, my parents decided to keep the breed spaniel as a family dog in the following years as well. (Mostly they were bitches, which were kept company by a male dog three times.) However, the family also included a Field Spaniel bitch once and currently a Cocker Spaniel lady again and a Beagle bitch.

In 2009, the decision was made to make the wish for our own dog come true. For us, the first step to owning a dog was a change of apartment, because dogs were not allowed in our apartment at that time. After the move, we thought about which breed it should be. We were also not sure whether we should have a male or a female dog. Your first own dog should be a puppy, in any case, we agreed. But there is much more to think about and plan before a puppy becomes a new member of the family. For example, we had no idea how to handle a puppy, the food and what "equipment" we needed, neither did we know how to raise him or how to integrate him into our work and private lives in the best possible way. Our first own dog should definitely be a big one, as we are both fans of bigger dogs. The decision was finally made to get a Bernese Mountain Dog, although this breed was not on the shortlist at first. But as life plays out, it often turns out differently than one thinks.

My sister had at that time a Bernese Mountain Dog which was pregnant with two puppies (one female and one male). Unfortunately, the female puppy died during birth, still in the birth canal, due to extremely unfortunate circumstances. The male puppy finally had to be brought into the world by cesarean section, so that he survived. Since there was only an interested party for the female puppy, but not for the male one, I offered to my sister that we would take the little one in with us. Merlin was 1 day old and still had his eyes closed when I held him in my hand for the first time. Yes, I was able to hold today's big strapping guy in one hand! And because my sister lived near us, we were lucky to visit the puppy very often and to experience live how the little ball grew up splendidly. In the meantime, there was still extensive research for the name (changing several times), and finally the puppy Merlin was "baptized." Merlin's arrival is now many years ago, and in November 2020 he celebrated his 10th birthday. We hope to spend many more years with him and are happy to have him in our family. He enriches our lives greatly!

Merlin's moving in with us

We brought Merlin home when he was 10 weeks old. Since we already had four male cats at home and we didn't want to let them and Merlin loose on each other, we separated the cats and the dog from each other for the first two days. We then let our tomcats into the room where Merlin had stayed before and vice versa, so the cats and the dog, as new roommates, could absorb each other's smell without any major complications.

On the third day, the time had come and we left them all together. At first, of course, there was a lot of hissing on the cats' side, and the four cats also started to flee. But one of them was - just like Merlin - quite curious and interested, and they sniffed at each other. This tomcat and Merlin are still best friends today. But the other males also quickly got used to the newcomer. After 2 weeks without any big conflicts, the living together was completely peaceful, and so it remains until today.

What you should do to ensure a positive encounter between cat(s) and your dog as a precautionary measure is to shorten the cat's claws, especially on the front paws. Cats with their pointed claws can not only cause painful injuries to the dog (which, in the worst case, can become infected), they can also stand in the way of a peaceful and uncomplicated life together, if your outgoing dog always associates the first encounter with your cat with pain. If you have a puppy, then you should also make sure that he doesn't "shower your cat with too much love" out of sheer joy over his animal companions. Your cat should therefore always have the opportunity to retreat from the puppy - preferably to a place that is inaccessible to the puppy (for example, a high scratching post with a lying surface at the top).

Educational measures we carried out

Merlin first visited a puppy school with us and learned there (playfully) about social contact with dogs and bitches of the same age. Afterwards, we changed to a young dog course, where he learned the most important commands like „Heel," "Sit," and "Stay." By the way, the command "Stay" is void if the previously given "Sit" is executed correctly. The dog must sit or lie down until the command is cancelled by you, for example, by "Run" or "Free." In a training course, the additional command "Stay" after "Sit" could even result in a deduction of points. With Merlin, teaching the basic commands with a lot of patience and one or two rewards worked quite well. A reward does not always have to be a treat; words of praise are at least as successful and should be used continually. But it must also be said that these commands are often quickly forgotten during puberty and you should be prepared to start all over again. After the young dog course, we had some private lessons with Merlin and a very patient, but just as determined dog trainer, both at a training ground and at home. The latter was mainly because we thought Merlin should get rid of the habit of pushing himself into the foreground every time we received a visitor, and jumping at the visitor. We were able to make him stop jumping. We were not consistent enough in "pushing forward," but it improved and is now at an acceptable level for us.

Contact with strangers

At this point, I would like to mention that Merlin, especially as a clumsy and sweet puppy, had a huge attraction to dog-friendly people and they constantly tried to pet him or touch him when passing by. This disturbed us very much and we told these (foreign) people very clearly to please stop touching and stroking him. In rare exceptional cases we allowed it, but only if it was asked beforehand whether it was okay to pet the dog. What should also be taboo is the feeding of any treats by strangers. Your dog should only be fed by you, and this applies equally to giving orders. No stranger has the right to order your dog to do anything. We had to point this out to some of our fellow humans every now and then.

Merlin's presence in the workplace

I am lucky that my employer allows me to take Merlin with me to work. On top of that, my parents-in-law support us because Merlin is allowed to spend the whole day with them every Monday during a working week. On Tuesdays, Merlin is then in the office all day, where he has his berth in a quiet place. During our lunch break, we always take Merlin for a long walk, which is good for him and for us. On Wednesday and Thursday, I work in the home office in the afternoons, and on Fridays, Merlin is only in the office half a day because we finish work at noon.

Walks and excursions with Merlin

When we are travelling with Merlin, we always make sure that we comply with any applicable line regulations. Since we usually use a rolling leash (Flexi leash), we always show consideration for other walkers, joggers and cyclists. This means that we bring Merlin to us and let him walk right next to us if someone comes towards us or overtakes us. In this way, there has never been any stress because Merlin has never blocked anyone's path. At the same time, people who were afraid of dogs were not put in an uncomfortable situation because Merlin was always close to us and we could react immediately if he made any attempt to run towards anyone.

In addition to the standard equipment in the car, there were always some dog excrement bags and an old bath towel, with which we could dry Merlin before getting into the car, if he had been swimming or if it had rained heavily during the walk. Drying also reduces a possible "wet dog smell" in the car. In winter, if you are out in the evenings along an unlit road or on a dark footpath or cycle path, it is advisable to wear something reflective, for example, a jacket with reflector strips, and there are also arm loops that light up as soon as they are illuminated by headlights. For safety reasons, we have additionally fitted Merlin with a light collar so that we are more visible in traffic and can be spotted in time. We also use a reflective leash so that we can be seen better when walking along a dark road.

Car trips

If a dog is taken along in the car, there is a range of possibilities. No matter which one you decide on, your dog should always be adequately secured. This means that he should not be placed in the passenger seat directly next to you or in the back seat without being secured. If you take your dog in the trunk of your car, then get a transport box or secure your dog by installing a separating grille.

We took Merlin as a puppy in the trunk of a dog transport box. When he was too big for the box, we installed a partition grille and provided him with the complete trunk. There are also different dog beds where a part of the trunk still offers space, for example, for your shopping. But we always put our purchases on the back seat when Merlin was sitting in the trunk. As already mentioned before, we organized a dog ramp for Merlin, because large breeds can get hip problems later. We wanted to spare Merlin's joints while he was not fully grown and his bone structure was not yet fully developed. We also wanted Merlin to get used to the ramp from an early age in case he needed it for easier access when he was older.

I would like to add something to the topic "to take along in the car," which is actually self-evident, but unfortunately still not all dog owners are aware of it. If you go shopping or do other things in spring or summer when the outside temperature is above 20 degrees Celsius, you should never leave your dog alone in the car. This also applies if you leave the windows open a little bit, because this has almost no positive effect on the locked dog. Even with slightly opened windows and a parking space in the shade, the car heats up quickly. To spare your dog any dangerous situation, it is best to leave him at home. You should also take this into consideration for other activities on days with higher outside temperatures, when your dog is in the car but cannot be outside with you. In summer, it is best to go for a walk early in the morning or late in the evening, when the ground (especially the asphalt) has cooled down again.

Longer car journeys

We took Merlin not only on day trips but also several times on holiday trips, but always by car. For this reason, I cannot give you any information or tips on taking your dog with you by train and air travel. We didn't want to expose our dog to a long train journey or the stress of an air journey, including accommodation in the cargo hold. Your dog will be very grateful for such a decision! For small trips and short holidays with Merlin, we always have enough fresh water, a water bowl and some treats or chewing bones with us. When driving for several hours, we also always make stops where Merlin can stretch his legs and do his business and get something to drink. During these stops, Merlin is always kept on a leash so that he cannot run away if he is startled by a loud noise or an unexpected situation.

No matter where you are going: before you start your trip, you should always find out what vaccinations your dog needs in the respective holiday country and you should have the vet check whether existing vaccinations are still effective. You should also find out about any restrictions on taking a dog with you and whether there are any muzzle-wearing requirements or other rules you must observe in the holiday country. Of course, you should make sure that you are allowed to take your dog with you when choosing your accommodation.

Holiday by the sea

We went with Merlin, among other places, once to Croatia to the sea, but have not repeated such a trip. Merlin had no problem swimming in the salty sea water (which was a first for him), but the heat was quite uncomfortable for him. We made a tent for him on the beach every day with the help of a wet and therefore cooling sheet, but it was still too hot for him. Thus, in the evenings, he always moved into the interior of the holiday house rented by us, in which it was pleasantly cool, due to the running air conditioning. In order not to subject Merlin to such a strain again, we did not make any more trips to holiday resorts where the temperatures were mid-summery. He accompanied us in spring and autumn, for example, several times to South Tyrol. The trip there didn't take that long, and besides, it was cooler and nicer there before or after the summer for extended hikes.

Water rat Merlin

Merlin loves water in case he can be inside it and swim, then he is a big "water rat". But with Merlin, there is also a little curiosity about water. If it rains, however, then he does not like to go outside, or very unwillingly, because the "wet" from above does not suit him at all. Another peculiarity is that Merlin does not run  through puddles of rain or water; they are always circled. We don't know why he does this, but it's okay, and of course we don't force him to walk through a puddle if he doesn't like it.

Please note: not every dog is enthusiastic about water and likes to go swimming. If you have a puppy, just take him to a quiet river or to a lake with a shallow bank and let him decide for himself whether he wants to go into the water or not. But you should never play with him and then throw a ball into the water, for example. He will run after the ball and bounce into the water without thinking. This can go off without a hitch, but it can also cause your dog to be frightened by the water and then be afraid of it in the future. This situation happened with one of my parents' Cocker Spaniels and made the dog shy of water from that point on - although Cocker Spaniels as hunting dogs normally have no problem with water. So you and your dog should take your time and let him decide for himself whether he wants to go into the water or not.

What we allow Merlin to do at home

We have allowed Merlin to do some things that some experienced and future dog owners may shake their heads at and not understand. I would like to say that each dog owner should decide for himself whether he would make our individual concessions to his own dog at home, or whether they are out of the question. In any case, nobody should feel obliged to comply with any rule or standard that might be implemented by a majority of dog owners. I think everyone should decide for themselves what they want to allow their dog to do and what not. We allow Merlin a few things more than the majority of dog owners do.

Place on the couch

Even though Merlin, as a Bernese Mountain Dog, is a rather big caliber dog, he is allowed to lie on the couch with us during our TV evenings. We have protected the couch with a blanket, and this blanket is also Merlin's fixed place, which he takes for granted on TV evenings. If this place is taken by one of our tomcats, then we clear the place for Merlin, because, despite his size-related superiority, he still shuns the space due to the defense by the tomcats and the unpredictable use of their claws. If you don't want to have your dog with you on the couch, just put the blanket somewhere else and let the dog take his place there. In any case, the dog will thank you very much if this place is at least in the same room where you are - after all, he would prefer to be near you, with his "pack."

Place in bed

Another permission concerns Merlin's stay in the bedroom. Merlin is allowed - in contrast to his cat brothers - to join us in the bedroom. We took him there the very first evening after he moved in and gave him a dog blanket as a place to sleep. Some people put the puppy in a kennel in the bedroom so that nothing happens inside at night when the puppy has to go out to do business. However, as mentioned in chapter 3, a puppy needs to "relieve himself" almost every 2 hours and he'll also draw attention to himself in the kennel when it's time (again).

Luckily Merlin was quickly housebroken and remained well-behaved on his blanket until my husband let him come into the bed once. This one time was enough for him to want to join us in bed and lie between us from then on. At some point we decided that he could do that if he wanted to. As Merlin grew older, we built him a staircase to get in and out of bed. In winter it is pleasantly warm in bed with Merlin, but in summer it is sometimes too warm. Meanwhile, Merlin climbs out of bed again during the night and then lies down on his dog blanket or on the floor - only to come back into the bed later. Of course, it is always a matter of taste whether you allow your dog to get into bed and lie with his "pack" or whether he has to stay outside and lie in his own sleeping place. In any case, I would always at least allow my dog to spend the night with me in the same room. I have the impression that Merlin feels comfortable doing this, and we (humans) like it just as much when he is not only watching TV with us but also when he is sleeping near us.

The special permission to be allowed to go to bed will not be granted to a successor of Merlin, because then we want to have a big dog again and such a dog already takes a lot of space in the bed. In our bedroom, however, there will definitely be a dog bed next to the human bed.

What is taboo for us

If we have Merlin with us when we go shopping, we always take the car and leave it there. We never set off on foot or by bike to go shopping and then tie Merlin up in front of the market. This is not just a precaution in case someone unties him or even wants to take him with them.

There are also some other events that can happen, such as the following:
- Dogs that panic and run away with the bicycle rack they are tied to, and, as a result, damage cars.
- Dogs that are kicked or beaten by people passing by.
- Dogs that are groped and hugged by children with the risk that the dog gets too much attention and snaps, or, at worst, bites.
- Dogs that are fed any kind of food that absolutely no dog should eat (because it does not agree with them or is even poisonous - see the chapter on "First aid tips" and "Tips for possible poisoning"). Apart from

that, I would not accept it at all that some stranger feeds or even just touches my dog without asking.

Regardless of all these unpleasant, unwanted and dangerous events, for some dogs, it can even become a traumatic experience. This is when they are tied up somewhere in an unknown place and left alone by their master (even if it is only for a short time). Therefore, it is best to spare your dog this possibly drastic negative experience.

How Merlin communicates with us

As mentioned in the beginning of this chapter, we got Merlin at the age of 10 weeks and we didn't know much about the non-verbal communication between dog and human at that time. But the longer you live together with a dog and the more you observe him, the more you learn to interpret his behavior. For  example, Merlin showed us already at puppy age when he wanted to get out to do his business. He would simply sit at the front door or the patio door. Sometimes he would tap his paw against the door, and, if we didn't react, he would make a yapping sound. With this, he showed noisily and unmistakably that he wanted to go outside. Later on, there was another clue, namely, that he sat down in front of us and started to „smack his lips", which also meant that he had to get out. By the way, this smacking is not only a hint for urgent business with Merlin, it is also a sign that he feels uncomfortable about something, as mentioned in earlier chapters.

A cause of Merlin's smacking can be a full anal gland, I was mentioning this topic in Chapter 7. The smacking of his lips can also mean that Merlin has a "bad" stomach and wants to go outside to eat grass. With the grass eating, Merlin calms his stomach, and the temporary indigestion is usually quickly over. Unfortunately, he does not always keep the eaten grass inside himself and this sometimes ends up with him throwing up inside the house instead of outside. You should not be too sensitive about the removal of the vomit, although the appearance and consistency is not very pleasant.

We have always used a dog excrement bag for the removal, and wiped up the rest with a few pieces of kitchen roll. By the way, a kitchen roll is a very useful and important item which you should always have at home as a dog owner - especially when taking in a puppy. If your puppy has done a big or small business indoors, it's also best to buy a spray that can remove the stains and neutralize the (urine) smell at the same time - very helpful to make the cleaning process really successful!

Another variation of Merlin's communication with us is that he touches our feet with one of his paws when he wants to draw attention to himself. For a certain period of time, he did the same when we were sitting at dinner and he wanted to get something out of it. In this case, we made it clear to Merlin with a clear "No" that there was nothing for him here and that he should let begging and tapping alone. The more consistent you are with "No," the sooner your dog will stop begging. The same applies to the variation that your dog puts his head on your thigh when you are eating. In this case, too, you should send your dog away from the table to a seat assigned to him or you should at least let him just sit next to you, for example, if you are in a restaurant or in a guest garden.

At this point, I would like to tell you a little anecdote. That Merlin is descended from the wolf, he proved to us several times during our living together - the first time this happened in the bedroom when we humans had almost fallen asleep. Merlin was already "dreaming," and in his dream, he suddenly started howling loudly like a wolf, which lasted for almost a minute. You can imagine that my husband and I were both more or less in bed at that moment with our hair standing on end, so frightened we were by the howling!

Speaking of dreaming: you will also experience it once or twice with your dog that he will process in his sleep what he experienced or "sniffed" during the day. It's usually funny to watch him twitch, kick or run lying down, or when he howls and makes some other strange sounds.

If your dog lies on his back when sleeping and stretches all fours comfortably, then this is a very good sign. That way you know that he feels absolutely comfortable and safe with you. Last but not least, I would like to reiterate that my tips and recommendations are based on personal experiences with our first own dog. However, no one should feel obliged to act in the same way that we have done. As individual as every dog, is also a life with him, and exactly this makes living with him so exciting and varied.

Closing words

So now you have reached the end of my guide and I hope I didn't cause too much of a chaos of new thoughts and considerations! It is just important to me to show you that one should never decide spontaneously and at short notice to take a dog in with you.

As you have read, there are very many topics that play a role in the planned living together with a dog. So you should also take a lot of time to think about them. It is better that you inform yourself comprehensively in advance and think about your decision carefully than take a dog into your home and then give him back sooner or later because you have imagined living together differently, because you do not have enough time or because you feel overstrained with the education.

Perhaps you know someone in your personal circle of friends or among your relatives or acquaintances who already has a dog of their own and already has experience. Then you can discuss any questions that may arise with this person personally and find out how he or she has fared with their first own dog.

However, you can also contact a dog school, a dog trainer, a dog breeder or an animal protection organization. The latter often offers the possibility to go for a walk with the dogs that are accommodated with them. This way, you can at least test yourself when walking with a dog. And at the animal shelter, they will be just as happy to take the time to answer your individual questions.

Please also consider that your dog will eventually reach an age where he is not so fit and agile. Then you should take this into account and not take him for extremely long walks or for trips that might be exhausting for him. And you should take into account that your dog might get one or the other illness and need special medication and more intensive care. But that should never be a reason to give your dog away - he will thank you for it with his unconditional affection until he walks over the Rainbow Bridge!

You are absolutely sure and have prepared yourself thoroughly for your new family member? Then your life together with your first own dog will be a great and unforgettable time, which will bring you a lot of joy and many beautiful moments!

PS: A big request for a small favor

For authors, book reviews are not only a helpful feedback regarding the work itself, they can also influence other readers. If you like my guide, I would be very happy if you give a positive review on Amazon - thank you very much in advance!

Research sources

(in alphabetical order, mainly German ones due to my origin and residence) agila.de / br.de / deine-tierwelt.de / de.wikipedia.org / doghealth.com / dogeridoo.com / erste-hilfe-beim-hund.de / fressnapf.de / hundeforum.com / hundeinfoportal.de / hundeportal24.eu / hundeseite.de / hund-als-haustier.de / inselhunde.de / media.uzh.ch / meinersterhund.de / nutricanis.de / planethund.com / senior-hunde.de / tieraerzteverband.de / tiermedizinportal.de / tierschutzbund.de / vetepedia.de / vetzentrum.de / vierpfoten.de / wsava.org / welpenclub.com / zooplus.de / zooroyal.de

Image sources

Private pictures with Bernese Mountain Dog Merlin (self-made by the author PhD Michael Schuerz or by his partner, the photographer and photo designer Peter Hinterseer: www.peterhinterseer.com). Pixabay pictures based on the Pixabay license valid on 1st of November 2019: All Pixabay contents may be used free of charge for commercial and non-commercial applications, printed and digital. The concrete Pixabay source information for each individual picture will be provided on request.

Imprint

Author & Publisher: PhD Michael Schuerz, Stettiner Str. 9, 83410 Laufen, Germany / Cover picture: Photographer PhD Michael Schuerz / Image editing Peter Hinterseer

KDP-ISBN (paperback): 9798768321840

Copyright

Printed in Great Britain
by Amazon

47619426R00066